Donna Kooler's
555 Fabulous Cross-Stitch Patterns

Donna Kooler's
555 Fabulous
Cross-Stitch
Patterns

Sterling Publishing Co., Inc. New York
A Sterling/Chapelle Book

For Kooler Design Studio, Inc.

Editor
Priscilla Timm

President
Donna Kooler

Executive Vice President
Linda Gillum

Vice President
Priscilla Timm

Creative Director
Deanna Hall West

Executive Assistant
Loretta Heden

Staff Designers
Barbara Baatz
Linda Gillum
Jorja Hernandez
Nancy Rossi
Sandy Orton

Contributing Artists
Donna Yuen
Pam Johnson
Holly DeFount

Design Assistants
Sara Angle
Anita Forfang
Laurie Grant
Virginia Hanley-Rivett
Marsha Hinkson
Arlis Johnson
Lori Patton
Char Randolph
Giana Shaw
Pam Whyte

For Chapelle Ltd.

Owner
Jo Packham

Editor
Leslie Ridenour

Staff
Joy Anckner
Malissa Boatwright
Kass Burchett
Rebecca Christensen
Amber Hansen
Shirley Heslop
Holly Hollingsworth
Susan Jorgensen
Susan Laws
Amanda McPeck
Barbara Milburn
Pat Pearson
Cindy Rooks
Cindy Stoeckl
Lorrie Young
Nancy Whitley

Photography
Kevin Dilley for Hazen Photography

Photography Styling
Susan Laws

Framer
Artist Touch, Ogden, UT

If you have any questions or comments or would like information on specialty products featured in this book, please contact:
Chapelle Ltd., Inc.
P.O. Box 9252
Ogden, UT 84409
(801) 621-2777
(801) 621-2788 (fax)

Library of Congress Cataloging-in-Publication Data

Kooler, Donna.
    Donna Kooler's 555 fabulous cross-stitch patterns
            p.   cm.
    "A Sterling/Chapelle book"
    Includes index.
    ISBN 0-8069-3183-3
    1. Cross-stitch — Patterns.
    I. Title
    TT778.C76K664   1996
    746.44'3041 — dc20   96-25869
                                        CIP

A Sterling/Chapelle Book

10 9 8 7 6 5 4 3 2 1

First paperback edition published in 1998 by
Sterling Publishing Company, Inc.
387 Park Avenue South, New York, N.Y. 10016
© 1996 by Chapelle Limited
Distributed in Canada by Sterling Publishing
℅ Canadian Manda Group, One Atlantic Avenue,
Suite 105, Toronto, Ontario, Canada M6K 3E7
Distributed in Great Britain and Europe by Cassell
PLC, Wellington House, 125 Strand,
London WC2R 0BB, England
Distributed in Australia by Capricorn Link
(Australia) Pty Ltd., P.O. Box 6651, Baulkham Hills,
Business Centre, NSW 2153, Australia
Manufactured in the United States of America
All rights reverved

Sterling ISBN 0-8069-3183-3 Trade
                    0-8069-6397-2 Paper

Contents

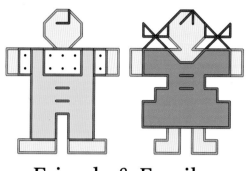

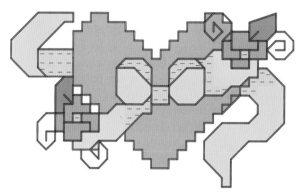

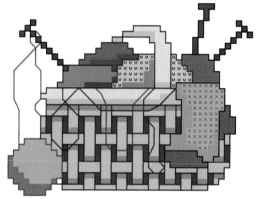

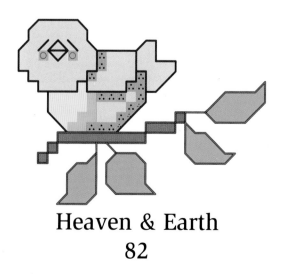

General Information

Introduction

Contained in this book are over 555 counted cross-stitch designs.

For each of the six chapters herein, we have stitched and photographed a sampler of several of the designs in the chapter. The individually graphed designs for these samplers have been placed on pages immediately following the photograph—usually the next four to six pages.

There is one color code for each sampler. This code falls on the last page of the individually graphed sampler designs.

The remaining designs in each chapter are not stitched nor photographed. Each page of graphed designs has its own color code.

To create one-of-a-kind motifs, vary colors in the graphed designs. The stitching possibilities will prove endless.

Fabric for Cross-stitch

Counted cross-stitch is usually worked on even-weave fabrics. These fabrics are manufactured specifically for counted-thread embroidery and are woven with the same number of vertical as horizontal threads per inch.

Because the number of threads in the fabric is equal in each direction, each stitch will be the same size. The number of threads per inch in even-weave fabrics

determines the size of a finished design.

Number of Strands

The number of strands used per stitch varies depending on the fabric used. Generally, the rule to follow for cross-stitching is three strands on Aida 11, two strands on Aida 14, one or two strands on Aida 18 (depending on desired thickness of stitches) and one strand on Hardanger 22.

For back-stitching, use one strand on all fabrics. When completing a french knot, use two strands and one wrap on all fabrics.

Preparing Fabric

Cut fabric at least 3" larger on all sides than finished design size to ensure enough space for desired assembly. If the design is used to embellish a project that will be finished further, check instructions for specific fabric allowances. A 3" margin is the minimum amount of space that allows for comfortably finishing the edges of the design.

To prevent fraying, whipstitch or machine-zigzag along raw edges or apply liquid fray preventer.

Needles for Cross-stitch

Needles should slip easily through fabric holes without piercing fabric threads. For fabric with 11 or fewer threads per inch, use a tapestry needle size 24; for 14 threads per inch, use a tapestry needle size 24 or 26; for 18 or more threads per inch, use a tapestry needle size 26.

Never leave needle in design area of fabric. It may leave rust or a permanent impression on fabric.

Floss

For each sampler and each page of graphed designs there is a color code. All numbers and color names on this code represent DMC brands of floss. Use 18" lengths of floss. For best coverage, separate strands. Dampen with wet sponge. Then put together number of strands required for fabric used.

Centering the Design

Fold the fabric in half horizontally, then vertically. Place a pin in the fold point to mark the center. Locate the center of the design on the graph. Begin stitching all designs at the center point of graph and fabric.

Securing the Floss

Insert needle up from the underside of the fabric at starting point. Hold 1" of thread behind the fabric and stitch over it, securing with the first few stitches. To finish thread, run under four or more stitches on the back of the design. Never knot floss, unless working on clothing.

Another method of securing floss is the waste knot. Knot floss and insert needle from the right side of the fabric about 1" from design area. Work several stitches over the thread to secure. Cut off the knot later.

General Information

Carrying Floss

To carry floss, weave floss under the previously worked stitches on the back. Do not carry thread across any fabric that is not or will not be stitched. Loose threads, especially dark ones, will show through the fabric.

Cleaning Completed Work

When stitching is complete, soak fabric in cold water with a mild soap for five to 10 minutes. Rinse well and roll in a towel to remove excess water. Do not wring. Place work face down on a dry towel and iron on warm setting until the fabric is dry.

Cross-stitch (X st)

Stitches are done in a row or, if necessary, one at a time in an area. Stitching is done by coming up through a hole between woven threads at A. Then, go down at B, the hole diagonally across from A. Come back up at C and down at D, etc. Complete the top stitches to create an "X". All top stitches should lie in the same direction. Come up at E and go down at B, come up at C and go down at F, etc.

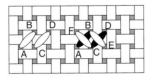

Backstitch (BS)

Pull the needle through at the point marked A. Then go down one opening to the right, at B. Then, come back up at C. Now,

go down one opening to the right, this time at "A".

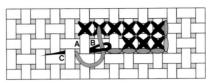

French Knot (FK)

Bring needle up at A, using two strands of embroidery floss. Loosely wrap floss once around needle. Place needle at B, next to A. Pull floss taut as you push needle down through fabric. Carry floss across back of work between knots.

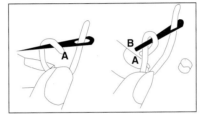

Long Stitch (LS)

Bring needle up at A; go down at B. Pull flat. Repeat A–B for each stitch. The length of the stitch should be the same as the length of the line on the design chart.

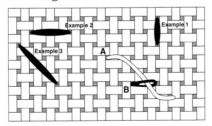

Lazy Daisy (LD)

Bring the needle up at A. Keep the thread flat, untwisted and full. Put the needle down through fabric at B and up through at C, keeping the thread under the needle to form a loop. Pull the thread through,

leaving the loop loose and full. To hold the loop in place, go down on other side of thread near C, forming a straight stitch over loop.

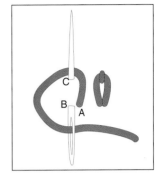

Couched Stitch (CS)

Complete a straight stitch the desired length of the design. Make sure floss is flat.

Make short tight straight stitches across base to "couch" the straight stitch (A–B). Come up on one side of the floss (C). Go down on the opposite side of the floss (D). Tack at varying intervals.

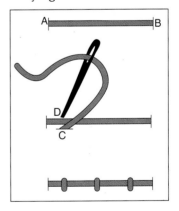

Flora
&
Fauna

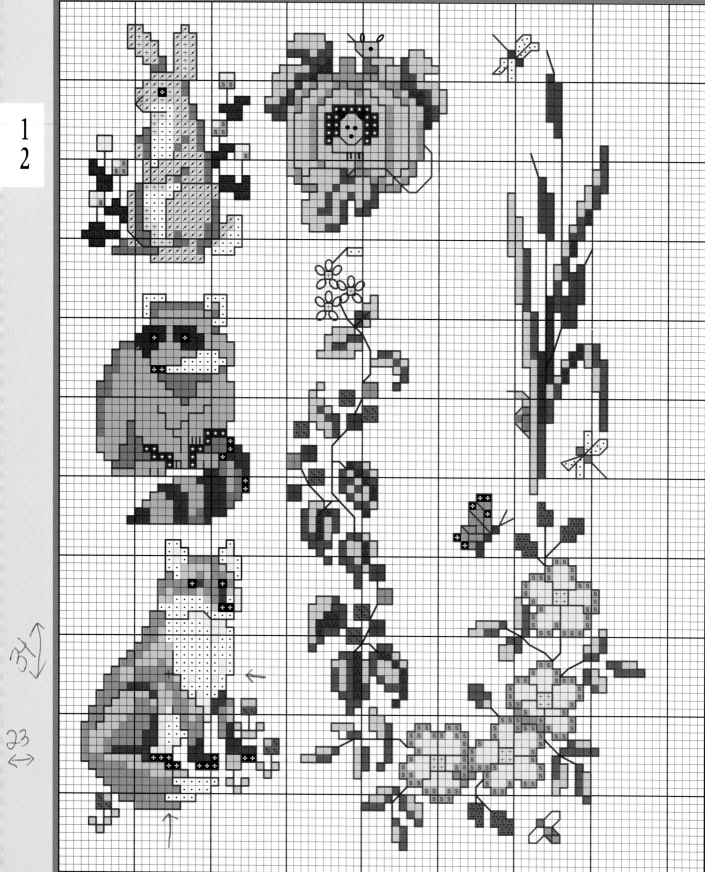

Flora & Fauna

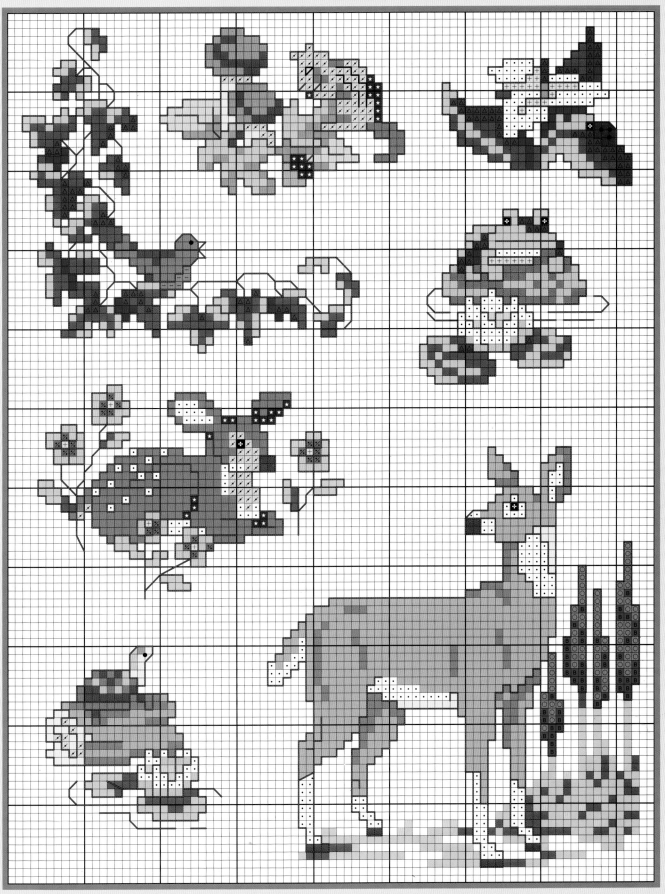

14

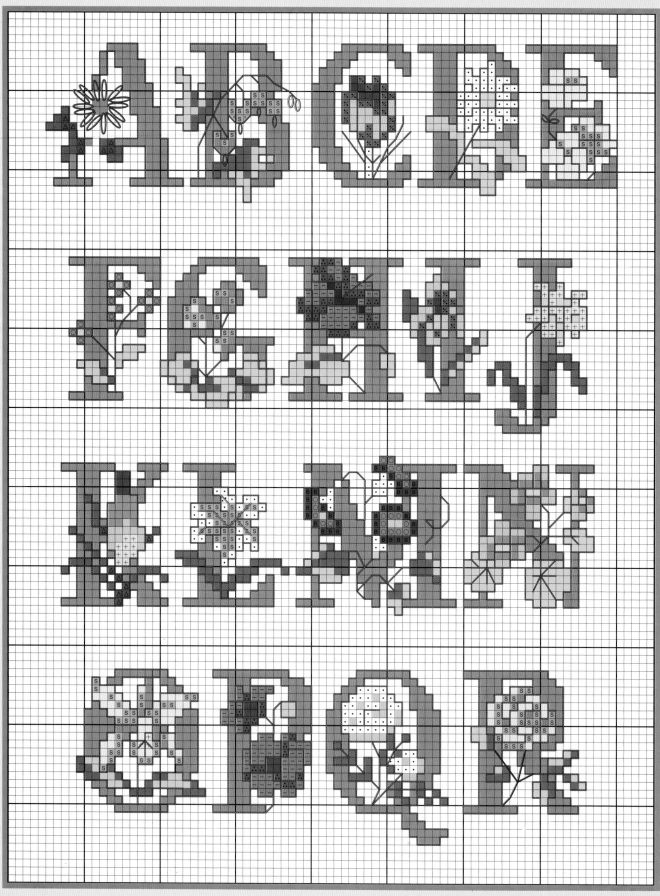

Flora & Fauna

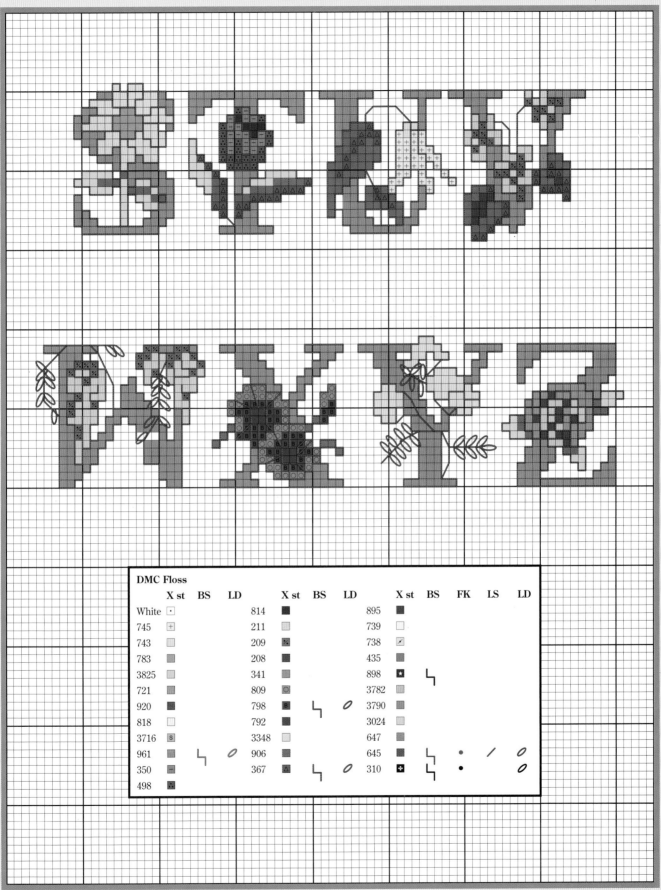

DMC Floss

	X st	BS	LD		X st	BS	LD		X st	BS	FK	LS	LD
White	·			814	■			895	■				
745	+			211	▨			739	▢				
743	▢			209	▨			738	◩				
783	▨			208	■			435	▨				
3825	▨			341	▨			898	✪	⌐			
721	▥			809	◎			3782	▨				
920	■			798	▣	⌐	∅	3790	▨				
818	▢			792	■			3024	▢				
3716	s			3348	▢			647	▨				
961	▥	⌐	∅	906	▨			645	▨	⌐	•	/	∅
350	⊟			367	▲	⌐	∅	310	✤	⌐	•		∅
498	▨												

DMC Floss

	X st		X st	BS		X st	BS		X st	BS		X st	BS		X st		X st	BS
White	·	758				498			564	S		704	E	310		
712		356		3743	+		562			561			702		3350		
743		3733		210			561			472			738		355		
741		3731		208			954			738			433			
3774	○	351		341			992	H		3828	N		452		
3779	×	349													

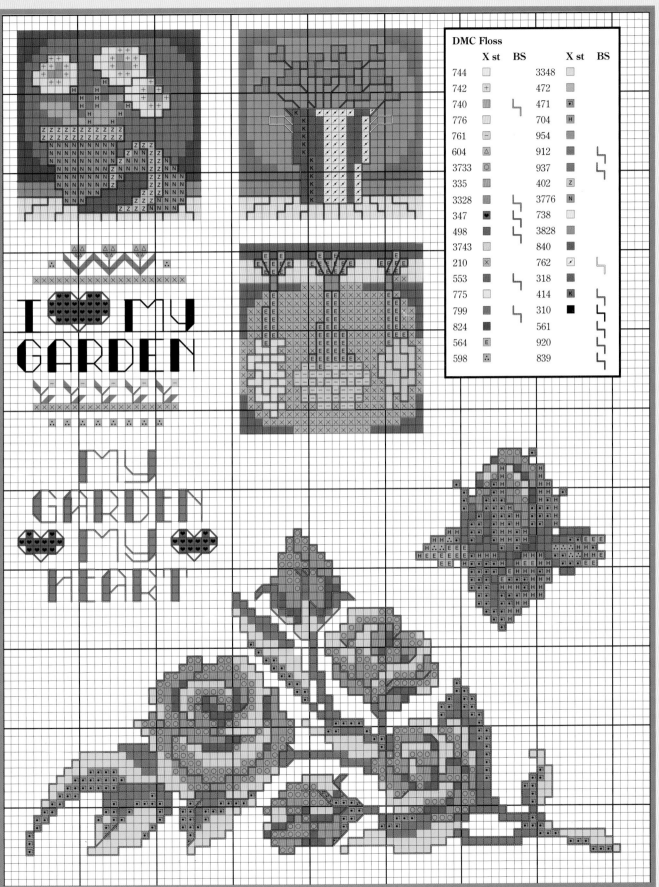

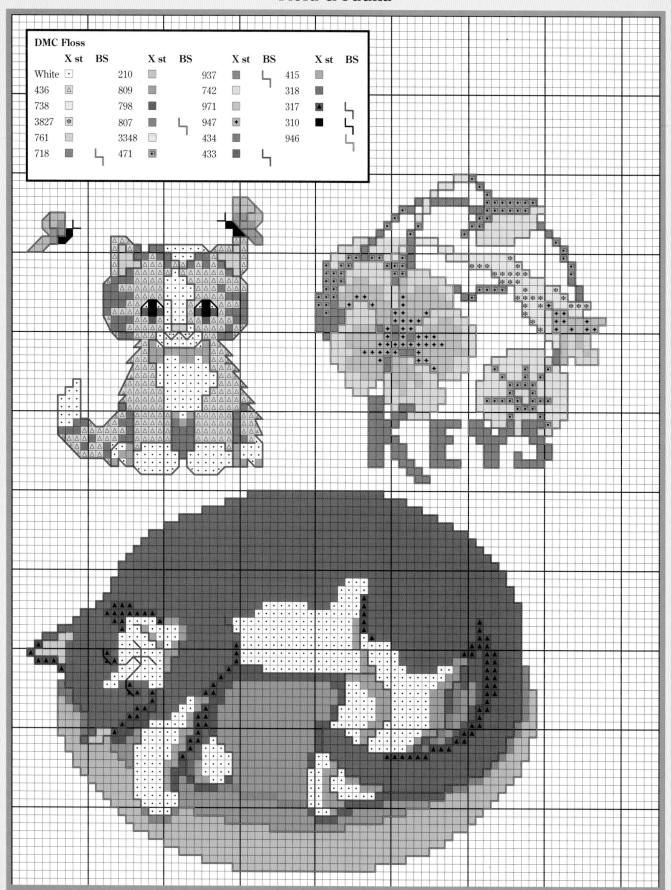

DMC Floss

	X st	BS		X st	BS		X st	BS		X st	BS
White	·		210			937		⌐	415		
436	△		809			742			318		
738			798			971			317	▲	⌐
3827	✳		807		⌐	947	✦		310	■	⌐
761			3348			434			946		⌐
718		⌐	471	⊡		433		⌐			

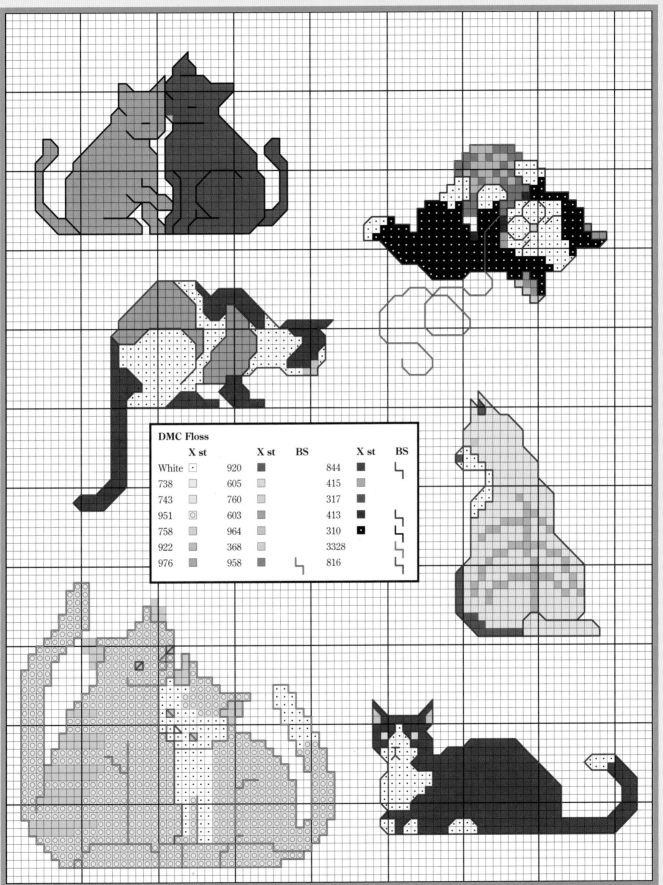

DMC Floss

	X st		X st		BS		X st	BS
White	·	920			844			⌐
738		605			415			
743		760			317			
951	⊙	603			413			⌐
758		964			310	■		⌐
922		368			3328			⌐
976		958		⌐	816			⌐

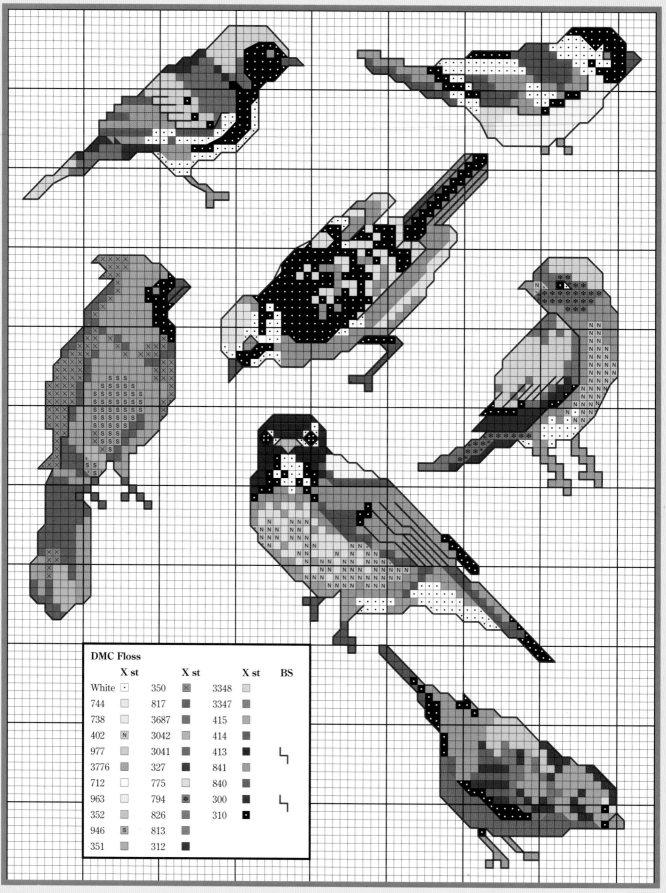

DMC Floss

	X st		X st		X st	BS
White	·	350	⊠	3348		
744		817		3347		
738		3687		415		
402	N	3042		414		
977		3041		413		⌐
3776		327		841		
712		775		840		
963		794	✳	300		⌐
352		826		310	▪	
946	S	813				
351		312				

Flora & Fauna

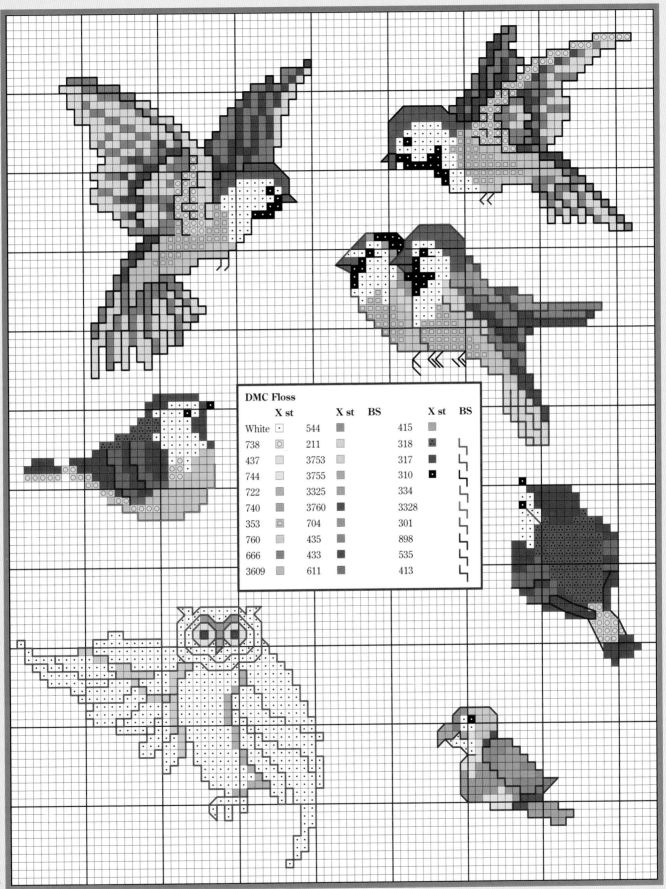

DMC Floss

	X st		X st	X st	BS		X st	BS
White	·	544		415	
738		211		318	
437		3753		317	
744		3755		310	
722		3325		334	
740		3760		3328	
353		704		301	
760		435		898	
666		433		535	
3609		611		413	

Flora & Fauna

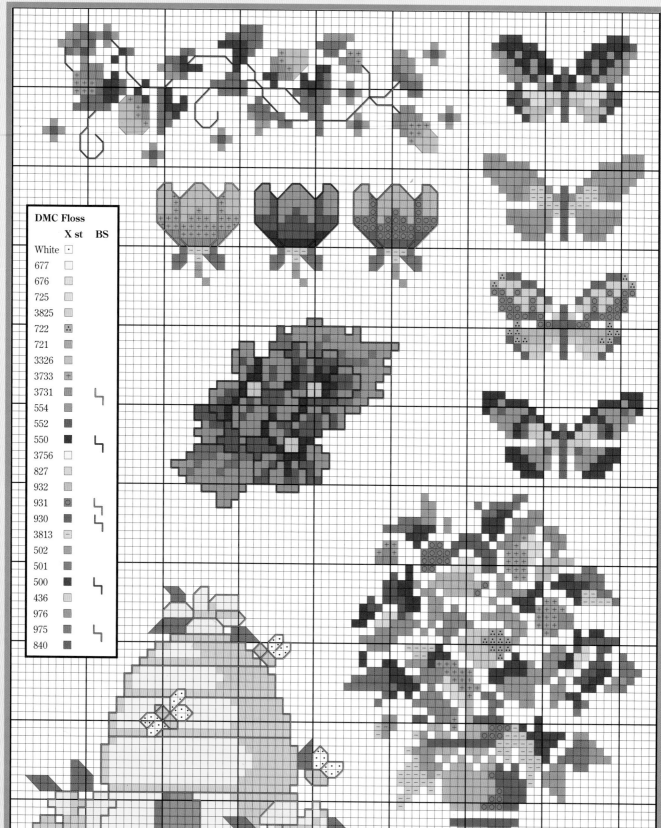

DMC Floss

	X st	BS
White	·	
677		
676		
725		
3825		
722		
721		
3326		
3733	+	
3731		⌐
554		
552		
550		⌐
3756		
827		
932		
931	◎	⌐
930		⌐
3813	−	
502		
501		
500		⌐
436		
976		
975		⌐
840		

DMC Floss

	X st	BS
White	·	
722		
721	X	
606		
321		
815		⌐
961		
3350		
772		
913		
910		
310		⌐

Friends
&
Family

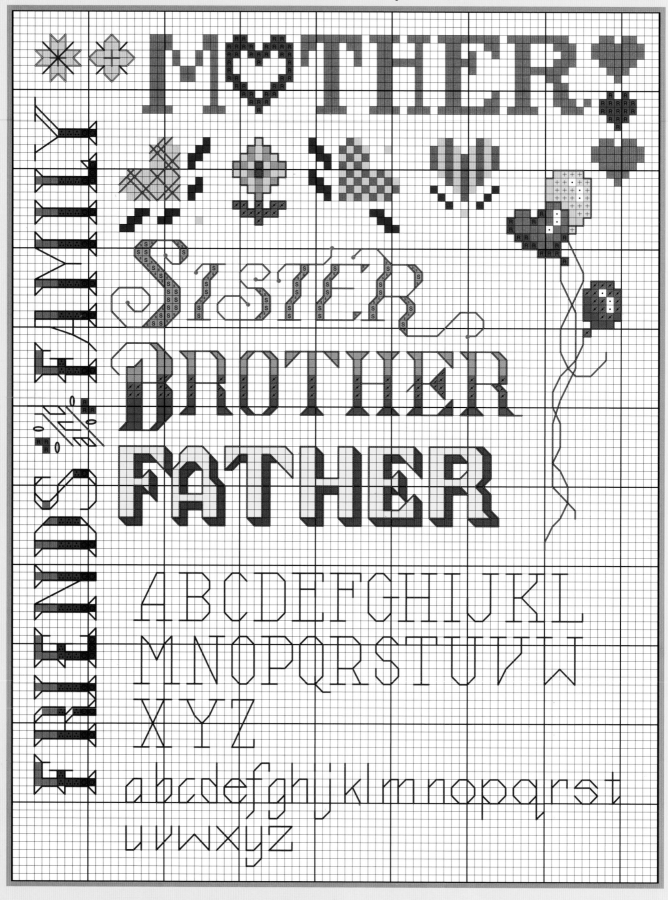

28

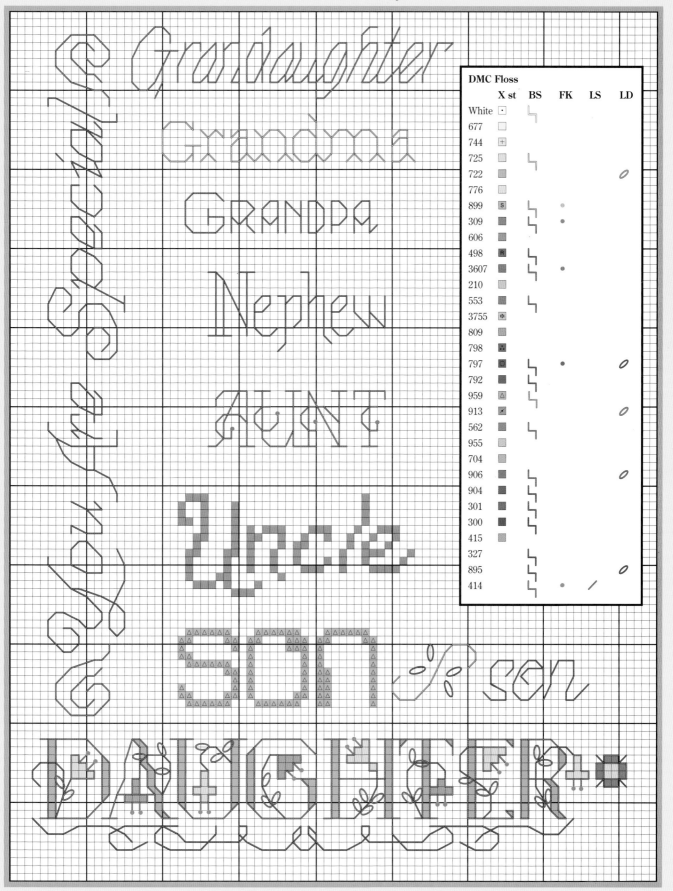

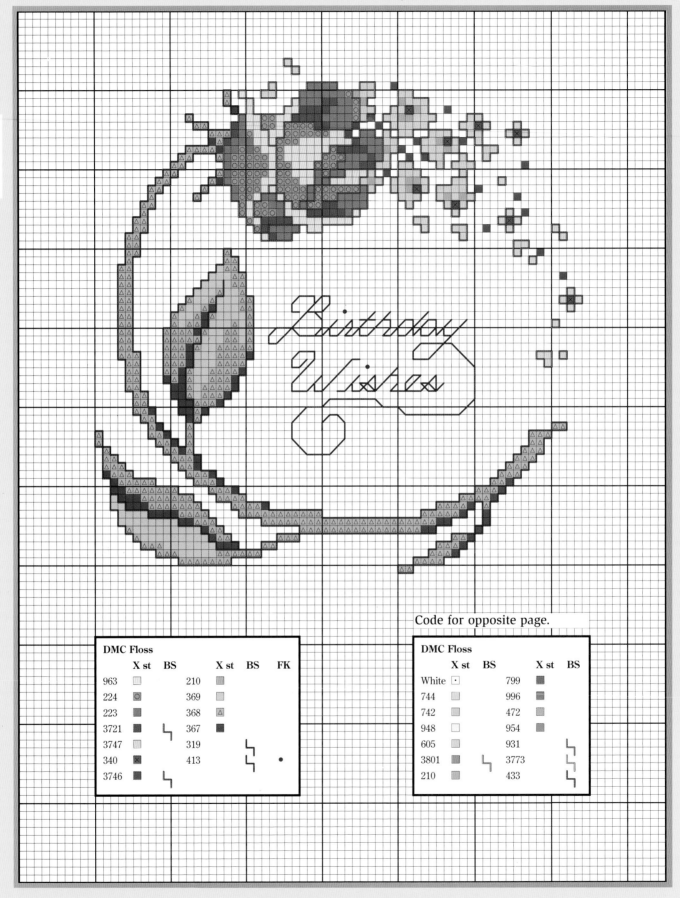

Birthday
Wishes

Code for opposite page.

DMC Floss					
	X st	BS	X st	BS	FK
963			210		
224			369		
223			368		
3721			367		
3747			319		
340			413		
3746					

DMC Floss				
	X st	BS	X st	BS
White	·		799	
744			996	
742			472	
948			954	
605			931	
3801			3773	
210			433	

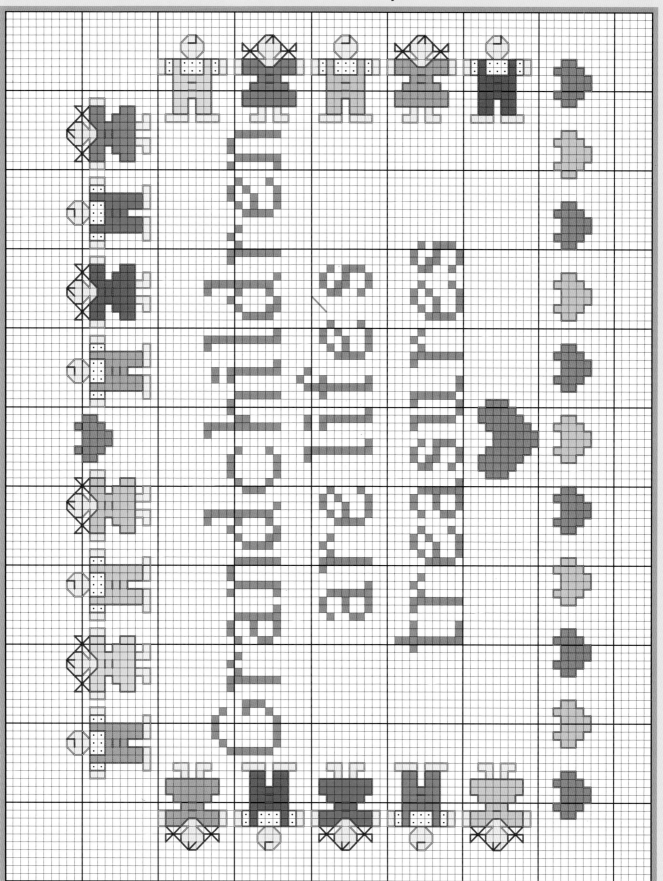

3
3

Mother

DMC Floss

	X st	BS		X st	BS
3078			498		
3821			563		
3820			562		
352			3787		
666					

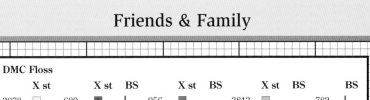

DMC Floss

	X st		X st	BS		X st	BS		X st	BS		BS
3078		680			956			3813		782		
726		776			747			3816		309		
972		957			3807			452				

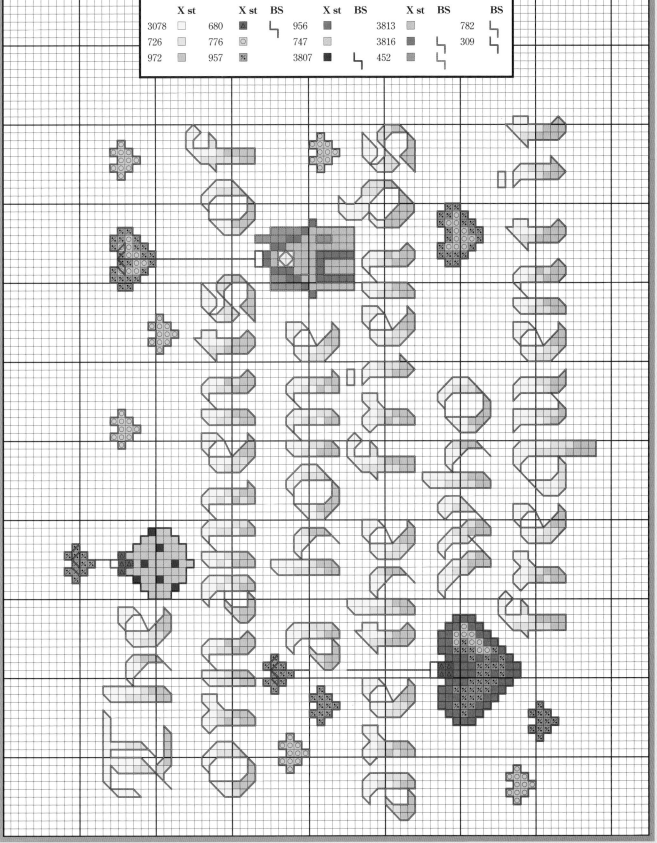

3
6

DMC Floss

	X st	BS		X st	BS	FK
White	·		3802	■	⌐	
712	□		775	▨		
727	▨		800	⋮		
743	◎		738	+		
783	▨		402	▨		
963	▨		3776	▨		
224	▨		318	▨		
223	▨	⌐	780	▨	⌐	
340	■		400	⌐		
210	▨		413	⌐		•
355	▲					

Friends & Family

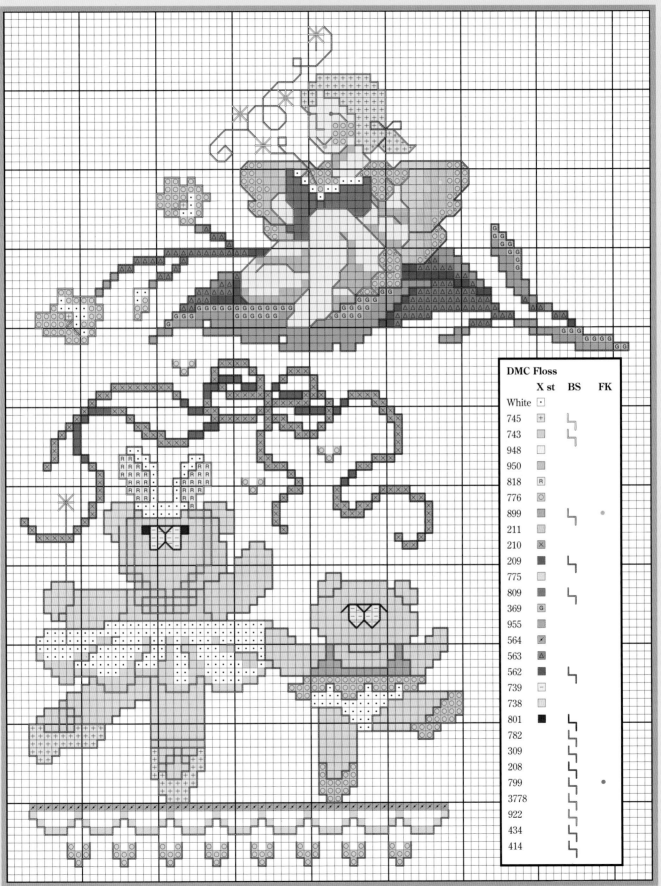

DMC Floss

	X st	BS	FK
White	·		
745	+	⌐	
743		⌐	
948			
950			
818	R		
776	○		
899		⌐	•
211			
210	✕		
209		⌐	
775			
809		⌐	
369	G		
955			
564	⟋		
563	△		
562		⌐	
739	−		
738			
801	■	⌐	
782		⌐	
309		⌐	
208		⌐	
799		⌐	•
3778		⌐	
922		⌐	
434		⌐	
414		⌐	

DMC Floss

	X st	BS
211		
209		
208		
3807		⌐
563		
3815		
3828		
610		⌐
3607		⌐
917		⌐
327		⌐
500		⌐

3
8

DMC Floss

	X st	BS	FK
744		⌐	
353	✳		
963			
3716			
666		⌐	●
210			
3607		⌐	
3325			
799			
702			
437			
321		⌐	
208		⌐	●
798		⌐	●
519		⌐	●
517		⌐	●
958		⌐	
700		⌐	
434		⌐	
414		⌐	●

Grandma's Treasures

If Friends were Flowers

I would Pick You

Celebrate! it's your Birthday!

The only way to have a FRIEND is to be ONE

Friends & Family

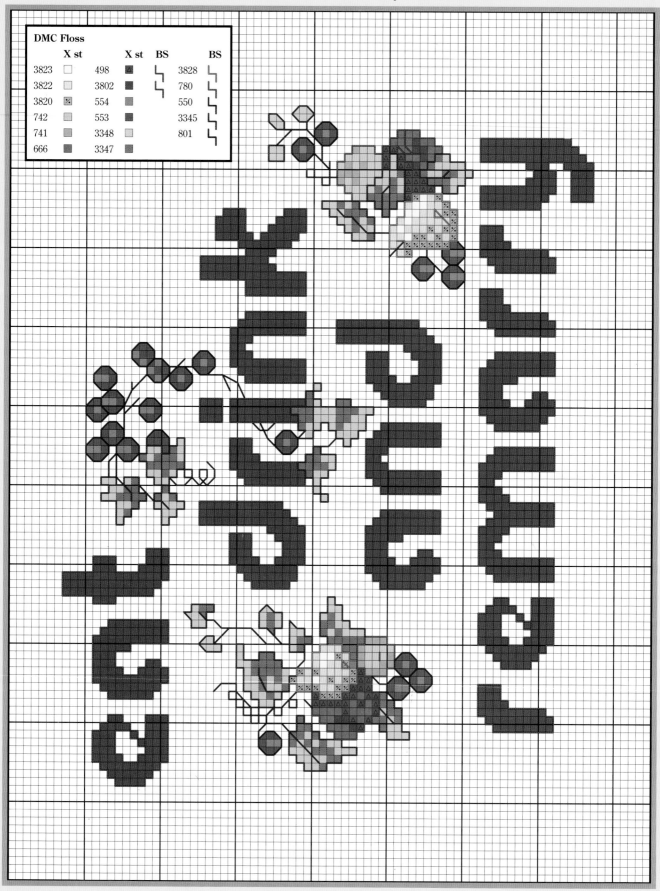

DMC Floss

	X st		X st	BS		BS
3823	☐	498	◤	⌐	3828	⌐
3822	☐	3802	■	⌐	780	⌐
3820	▨	554	■		550	⌐
742	☐	553	■		3345	⌐
741	■	3348	☐		801	⌐
666	■	3347	■			

40

Friends & Family

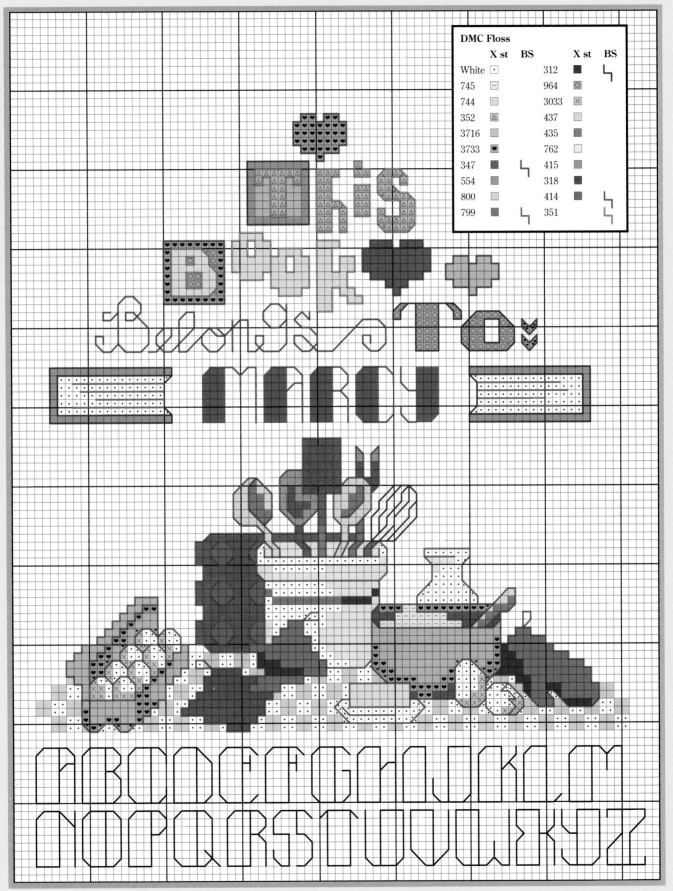

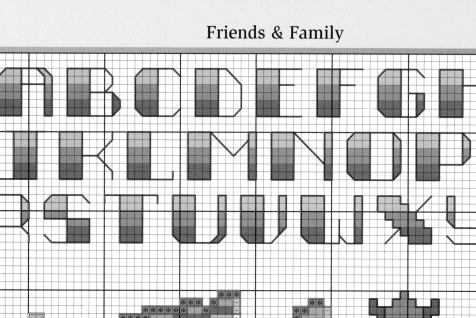

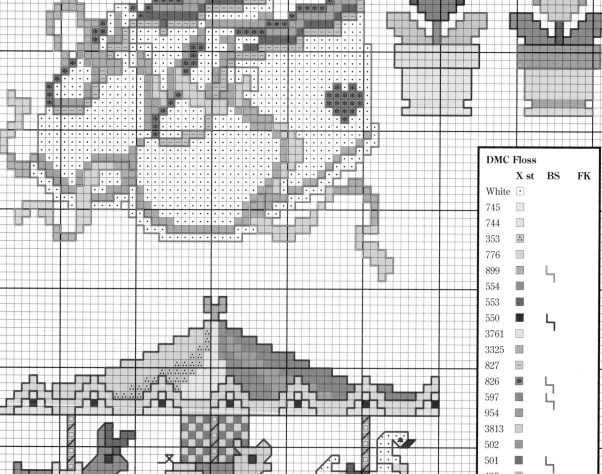

DMC Floss			
	X st	BS	FK
White	·		
745			
744			
353			
776			
899		⌐	
554			
553			
550		⌐	
3761			
3325			
827			
826		⌐	
597		⌐	
954			
3813			
502			
501		⌐	
437			
3031		⌐	
415			
414		⌐	
500		⌐	•
3799		⌐	•

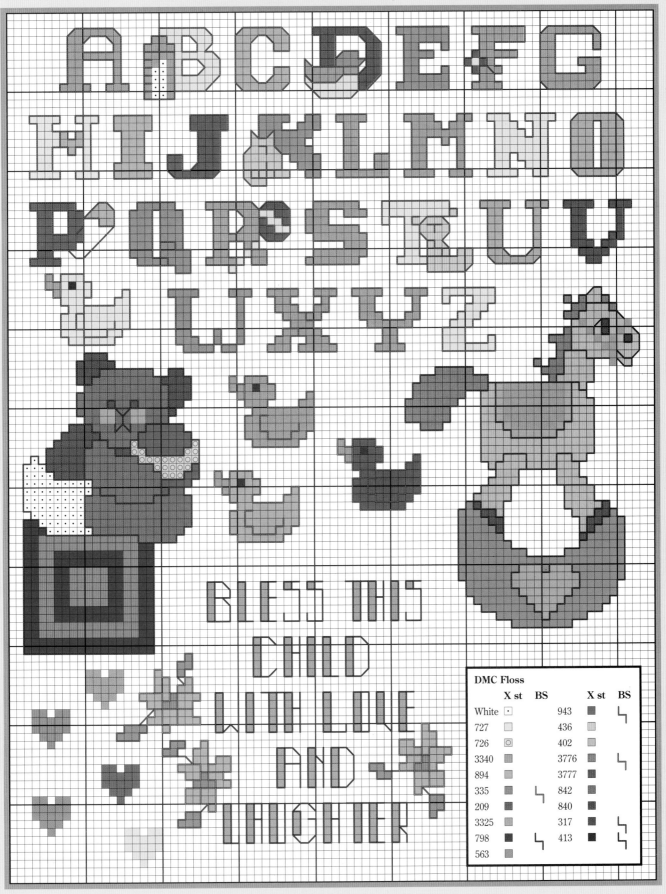

ABCDEFG
HIJKLMNO
PQRSTUV
WXYZ

BLESS THIS
CHILD
WITH LOVE
AND
LAUGHTER

DMC Floss				
	X st	BS	X st	BS
White	·		943	↳
727			436	
726	⊙		402	
3340			3776	↳
894			3777	
335		↳	842	
209			840	
3325			317	↳
798		↳	413	↳
563				

4
3

Heart
&
Soul

44

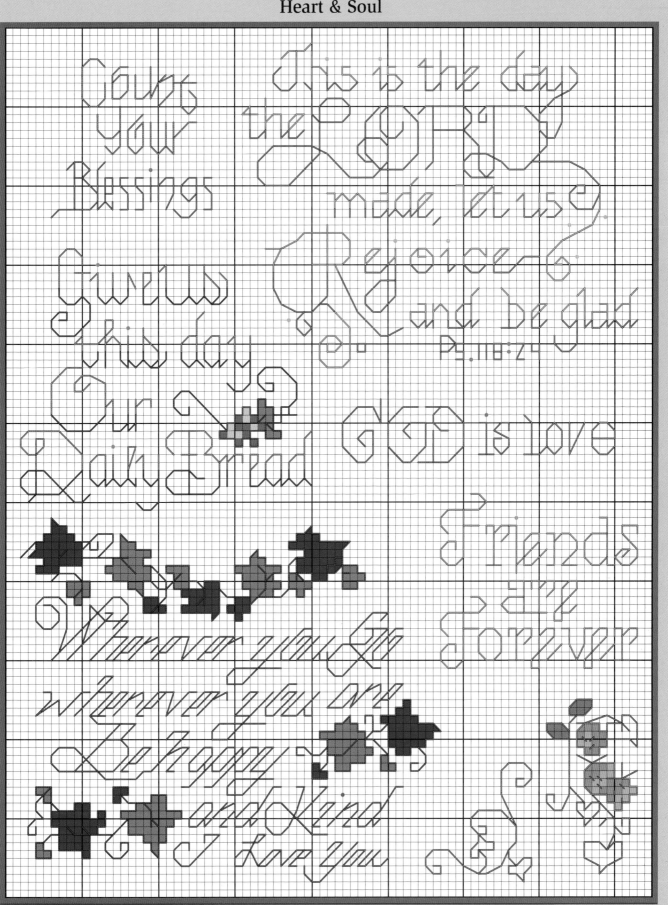

48

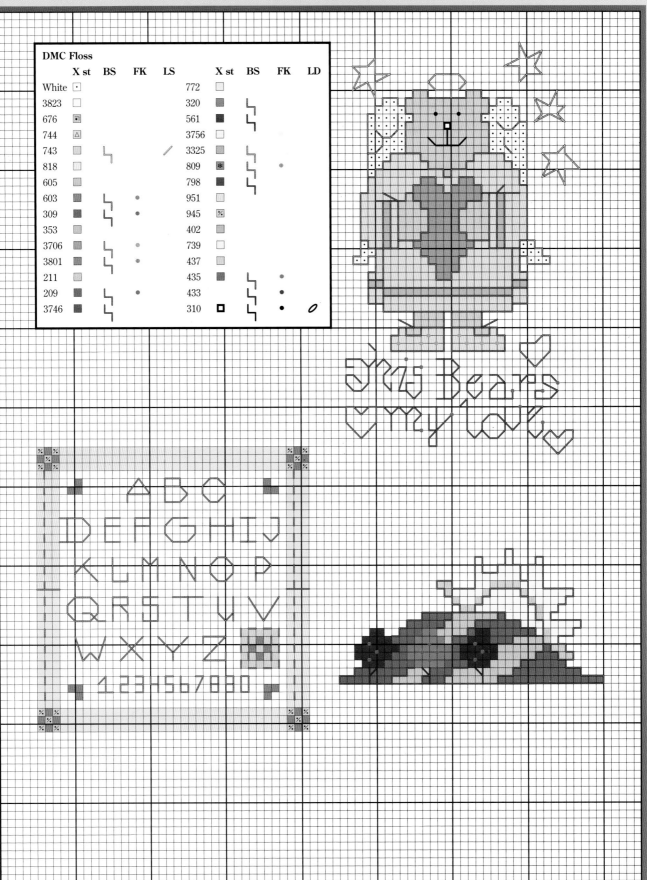

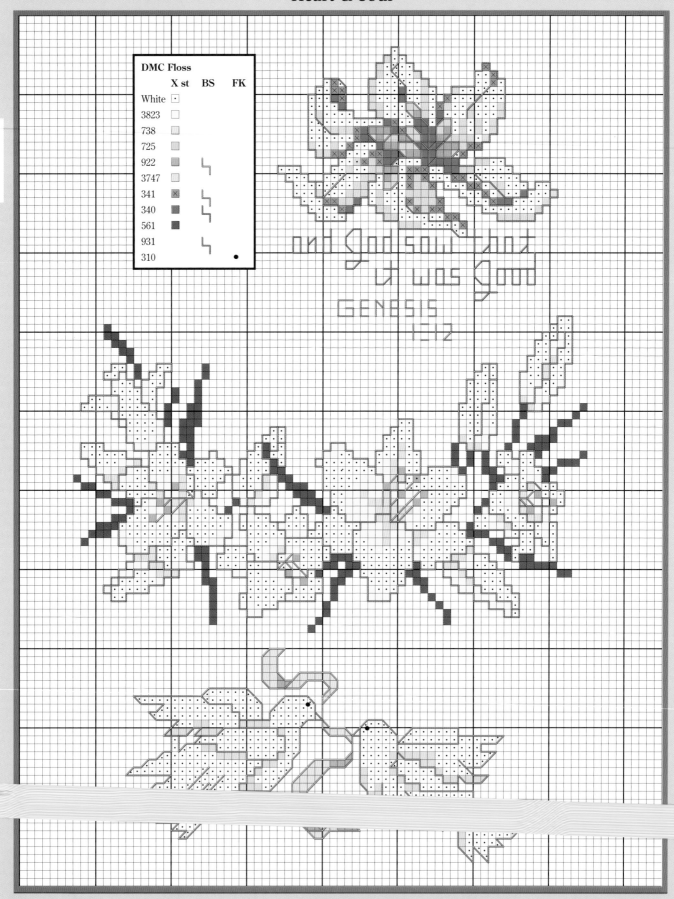

DMC Floss

	X st	BS	FK
White	·		
3823			
738			
725			
922		⌐	
3747			
341	✕	⌐	
340		⌐	
561			
931		⌐	
310			●

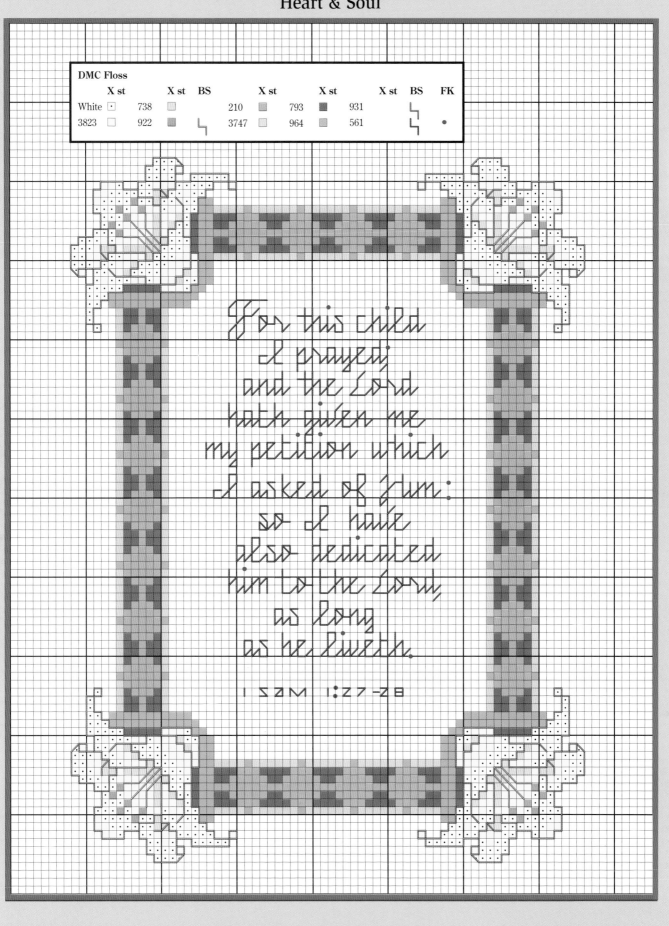

DMC Floss

	X st	BS	FK
White	·		
676			
745			
741			
605			
603		⌐	•
600		⌐	
211			
210			
341	+		
799			•
3347			
3345		⌐	
758			
780		⌐	•
310		⌐	

52

DMC Floss

	X st	BS		X st	BS
727	○		562	★	
725			986		
957			3760		
956	◁		781		
326			413		
563					

5
3

DMC Floss

	X st	BS		X st	BS
White	·		561		⌐
744			3348		
353			3347	✳	
351		⌐	3346	△	⌐
818	R		3345		⌐
899			341		
309		⌐	793		
563			415		
562			844		⌐

LET THE HEAVENS
REJOICE
LET THE EARTH BE
GLAD...
PSALMS 96:11

5
5

Heart & Soul

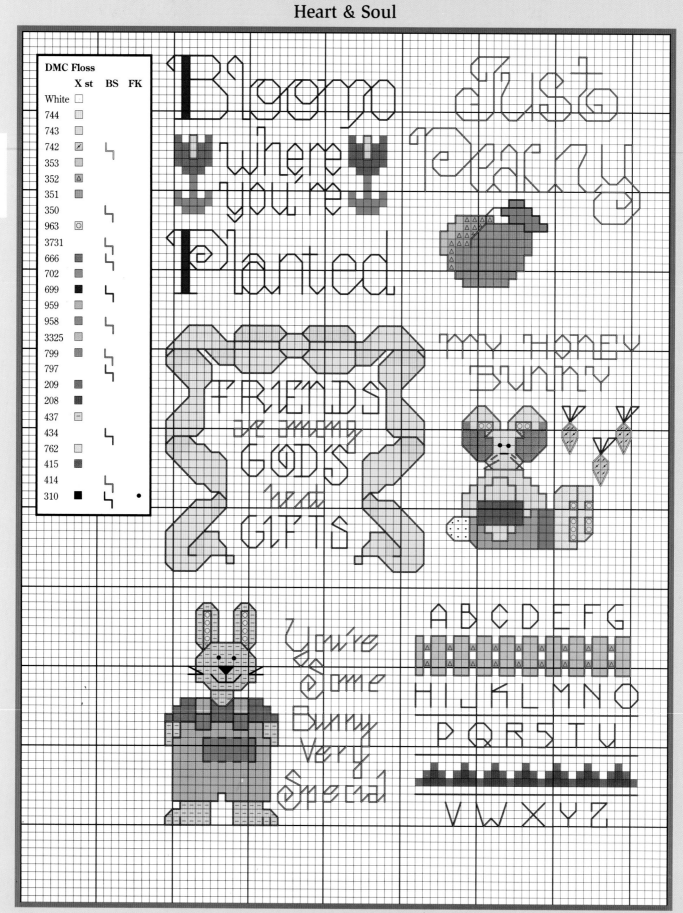

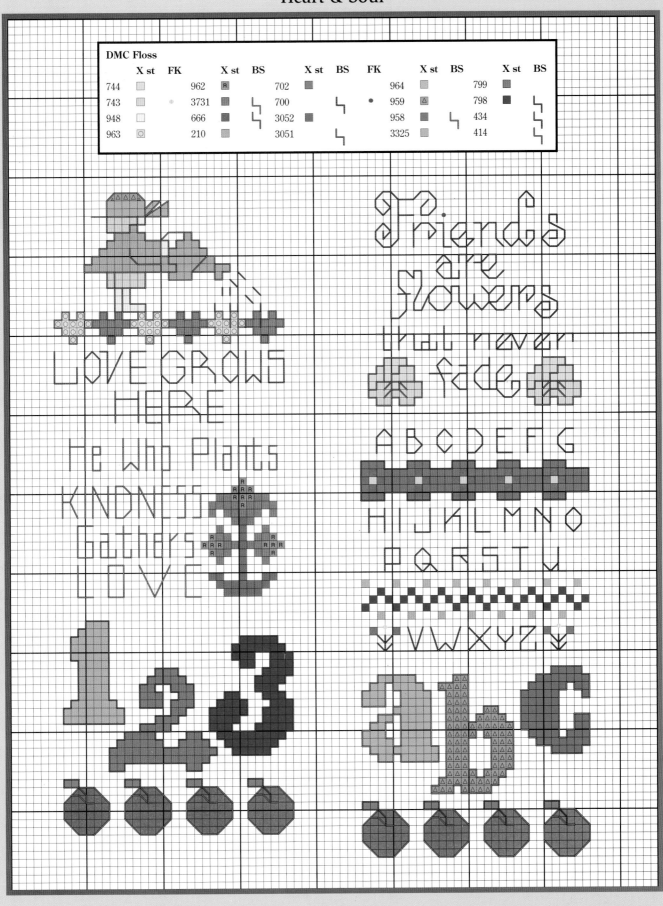

DMC Floss

	X st	FK		X st	BS		X st	BS	FK		X st	BS		X st	BS
744			962	R		702				964			799		
743		●	3731		⌐	700		⌐	●	959	△		798		⌐
948			666			3052		⌐		958		⌐	434		⌐
963	◎		210			3051		⌐		3325			414		⌐

DMC Floss

	X st	BS	FK
White	·		
745			
744			
743			
3716			
3731		⌐	•
321			
3609			
3608	♥		
3607		⌐	
210		⌐	
209		⌐	
704		⌐	
702		⌐	
959	⊙		
3325			
799		⌐	•
783		⌐	
435		⌐	
414		⌐	
310	✦	⌐	•

58

DMC Floss

	X st	BS	FK
White	·		
744			
743		⌐	
353		⌐	
818			
3716		⌐	·
3731		⌐	
321		⌐	
3609		⌐	
954		⌐	
964			
959	◎		
958		⌐	
3761			
3325			
517		⌐	
798		⌐	
739			
738			
783			
780		⌐	
414		⌐	

5
9

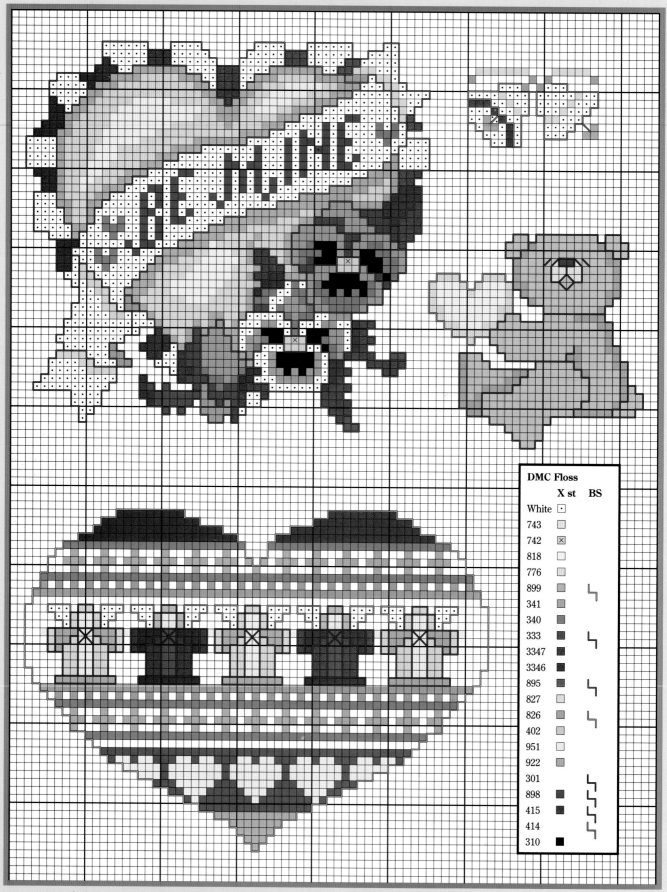

DMC Floss		
	X st	BS
White	·	
743		
742	⊠	
818		
776		
899		⌐
341		
340		
333		⌐
3347		
3346		
895		⌐
827		
826		⌐
402		
951		
922		
301		⌐
898		⌐
415		⌐
414		⌐
310	■	

Heart & Soul

DMC Floss

	X st	BS	LS
White	·		
3047			
677			
945			
758	◪		
352			
350	◎	⌐	
776			
666			
498		⌐	
211			
209		⌐	
775			
799		⌐	
798			
3347			
3345		⌐	/
402			
400		⌐	/
922			
920			
762			
317		⌐	
310			

Hearth
&
Home

Hearth & Home

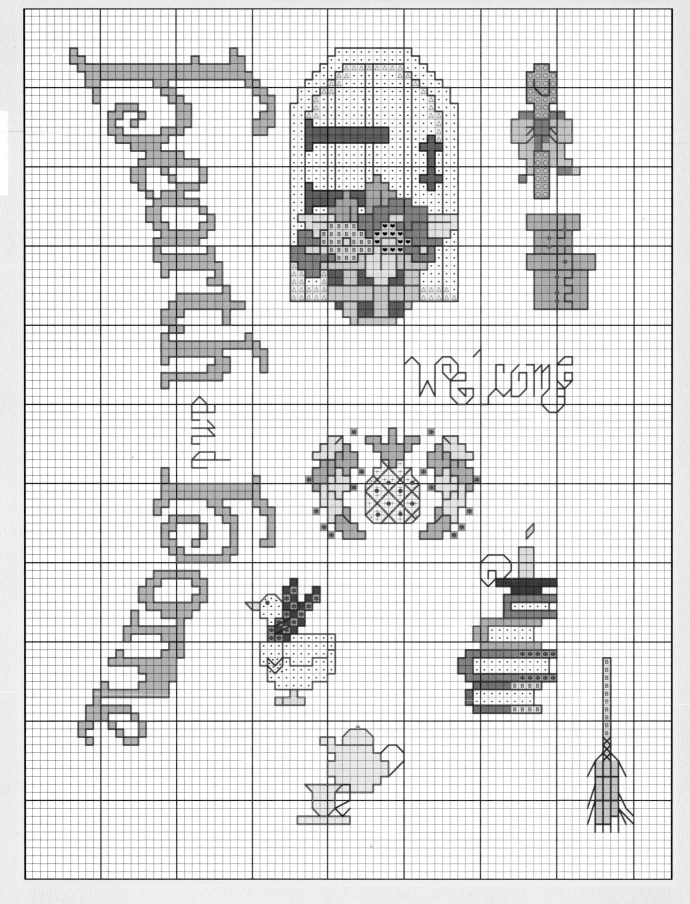

Hearth & Home

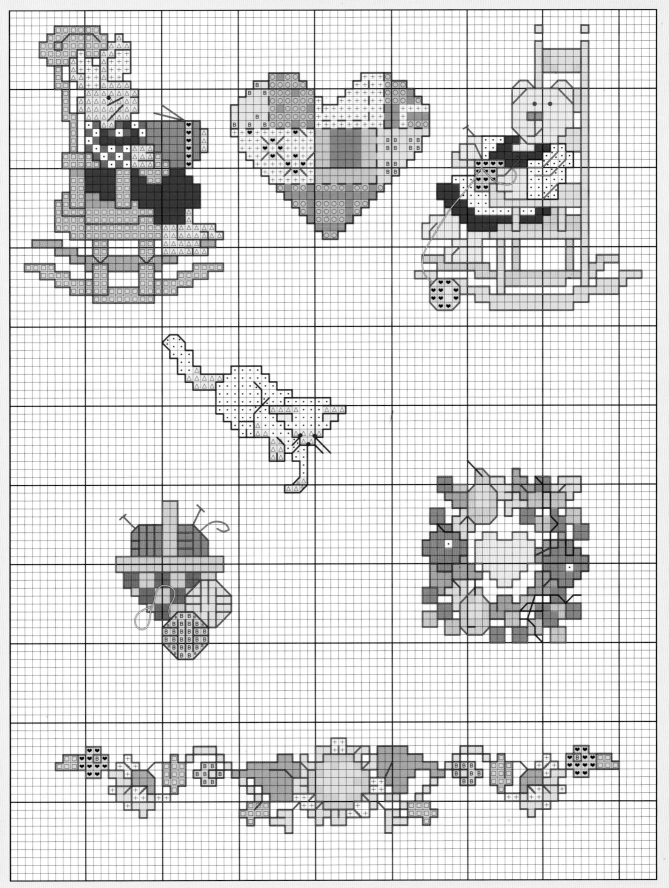

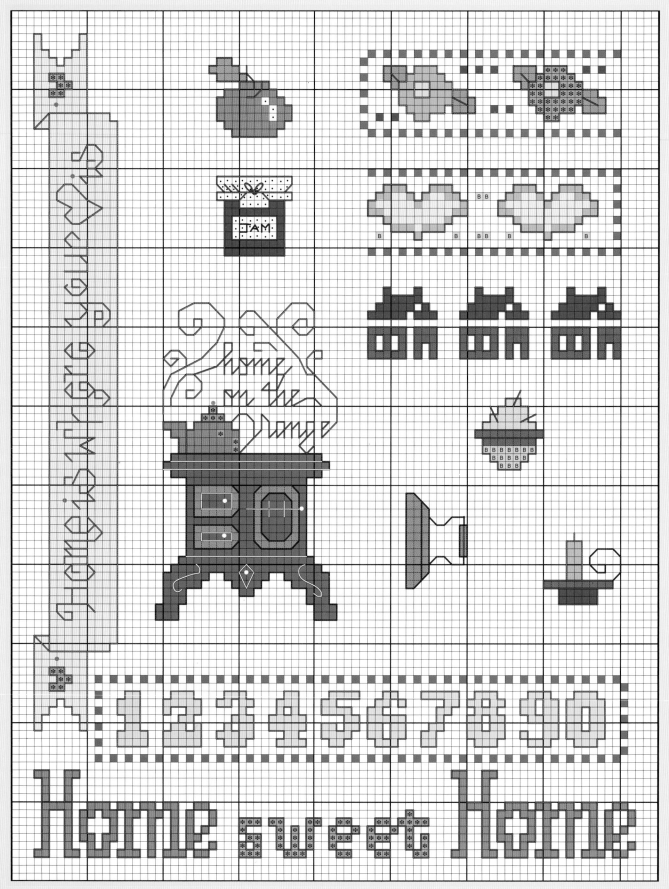

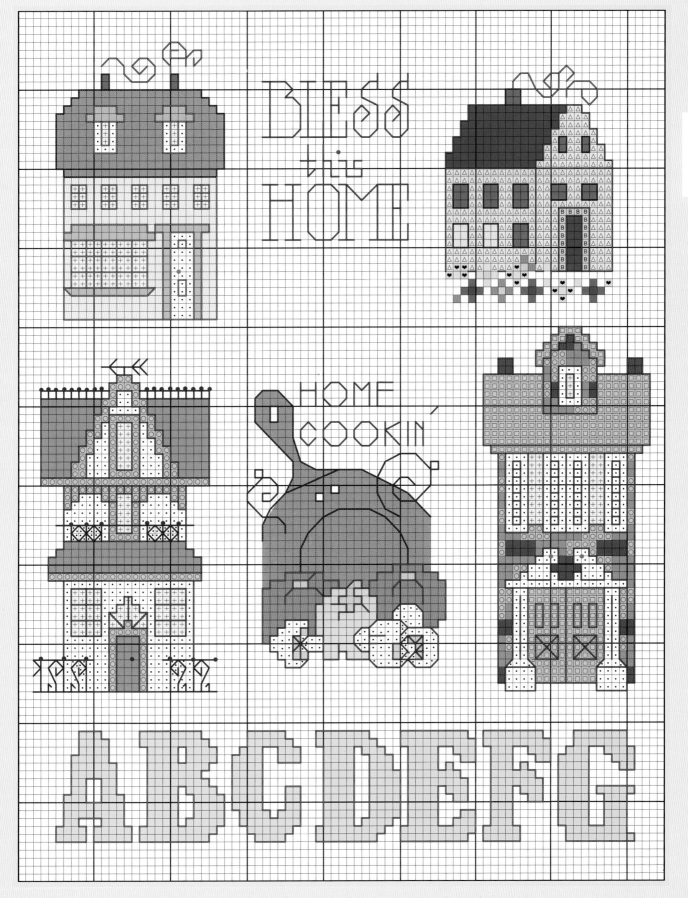

Hearth & Home

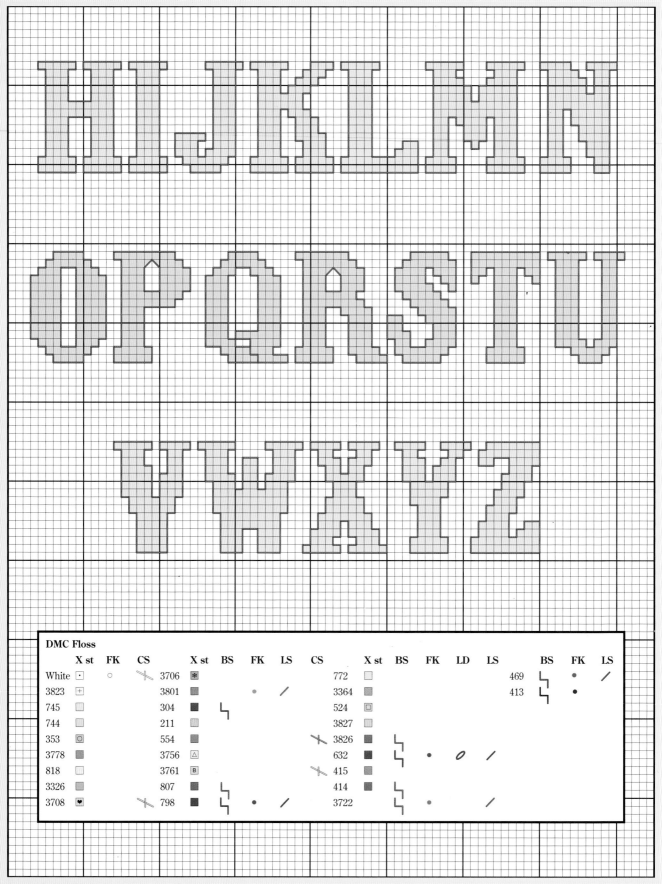

DMC Floss

	X st	FK	CS		X st	BS	FK	LS	CS		X st	BS	FK	LD	LS		BS	FK	LS
White	·	○	✕	3706	✳					772						469	⌐	•	/
3823	+			3801	▦		•	/		3364	▦					413	⌐	•	
745	▢			304	▦	⌐				524	▣								
744	▦			211	▨					3827	▦								
353	◎			554	▦				✕	3826	▦	⌐							
3778	▦			3756	△					632	▦	⌐	•	⬭	/				
818	▨			3761	Ⓑ				✕	415	▦								
3326	▦			807	▦	⌐		/		414	▦	⌐							
3708	♥		✕	798	▦	⌐	•	/		3722	▦	⌐	•		/				

DMC Floss

	X st	BS		X st	BS	FK
744	·		826			
725			954			
666	◄		824		L	·
498		L	400		L	
208						

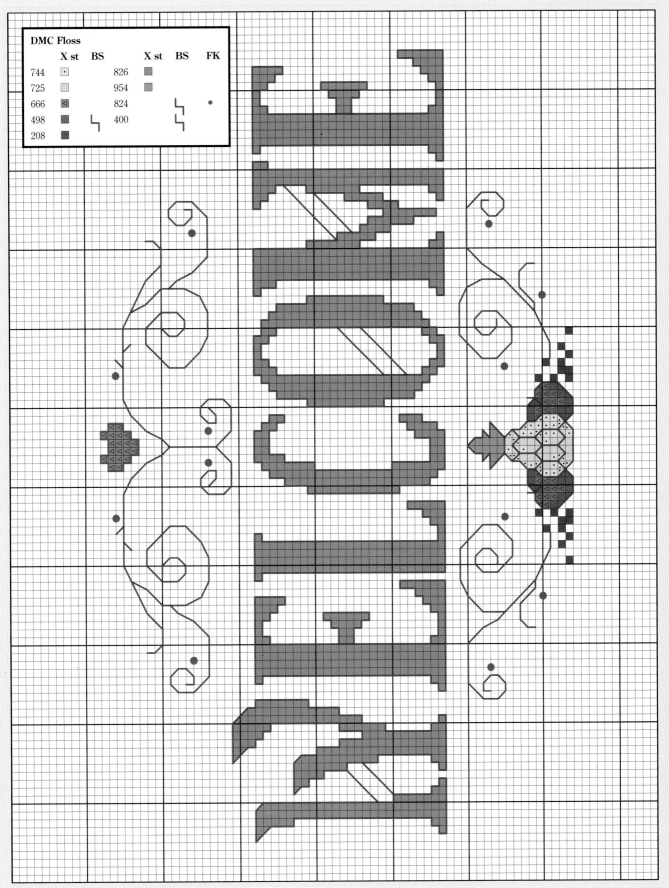

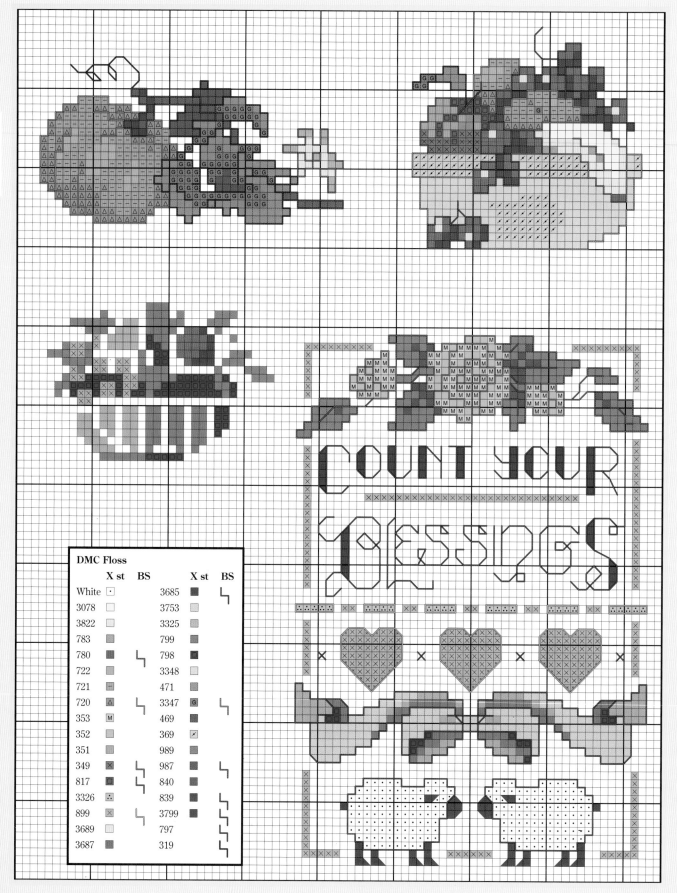

Hearth & Home

DMC Floss

	X st	BS	FK	LS
White	·			
746				
3078	△		○	
3827				
3776				
776		⌐		
309		⌐	•	
321	♥	⌐		
775			○	
3814				
738				
841				
801		⌐	•	/
838	◙			
415				
414		⌐		

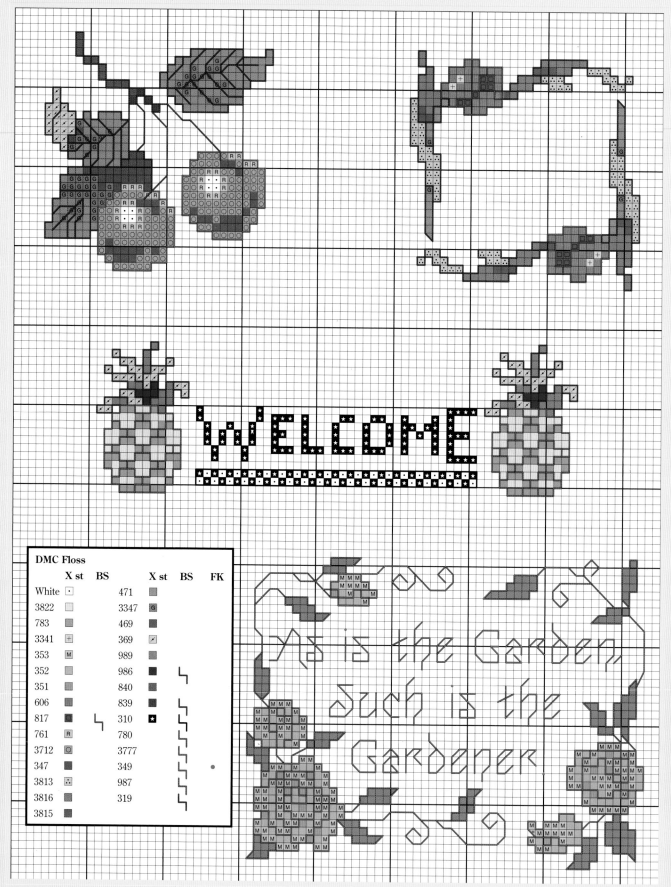

DMC Floss

	X st	FK		X st		X st	BS		X st	BS		X st	BS		X st	BS		X st	BS		X st	BS	FK
White	·		3341		304		★		772			3787			433			414					
746	⊙		818		606				704			437			453			3799					
3078		○	776	△	3777	N			904			435			762	⊠		310	□			•
742			335	H	800				3033			434	B		318			792					
971			893		794				3032														

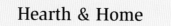

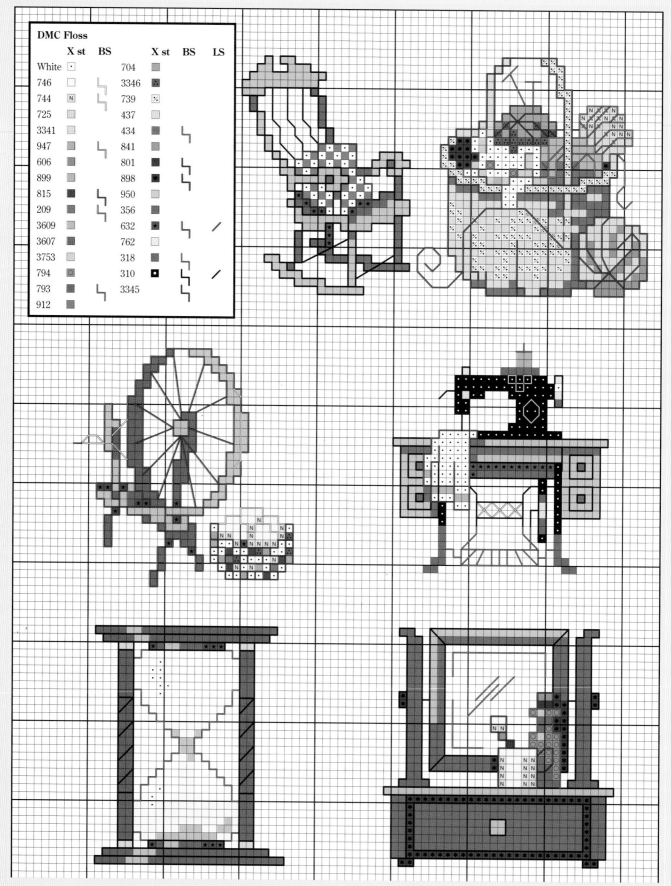

DMC Floss

	X st	BS		X st	BS	LS
White	·		704			
746		⌐	3346	▦		
744	N		739	⊠		
725			437			
3341			434		⌐	
947		⌐	841			
606			801		⌐	
899			898	✳	⌐	
815		⌐	950			
209		⌐	356			
3609			632	✳	⌐	/
3607			762			
3753			318		⌐	
794	◉		310	◘	⌐	/
793		⌐	3345		⌐	
912						

Hearth & Home

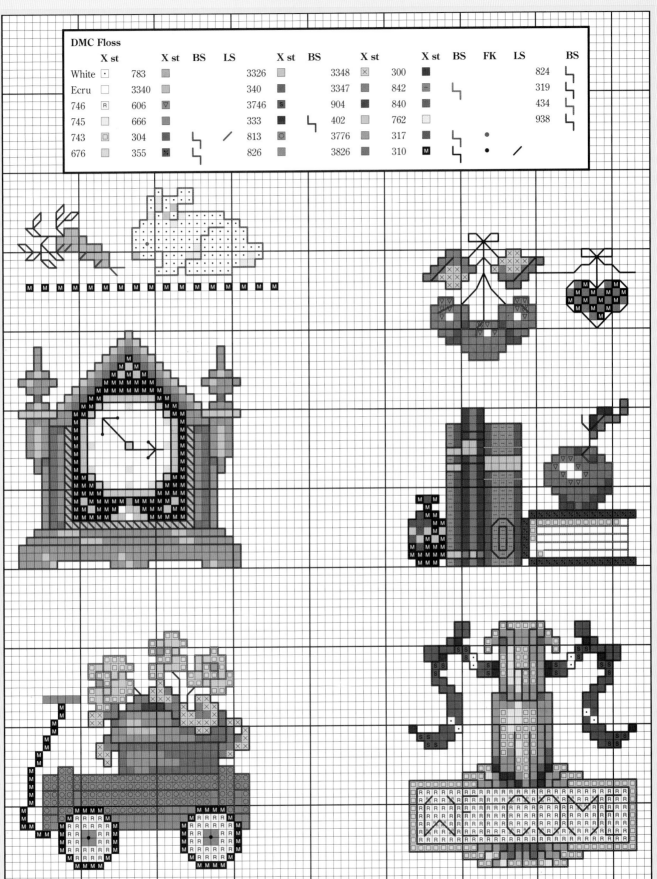

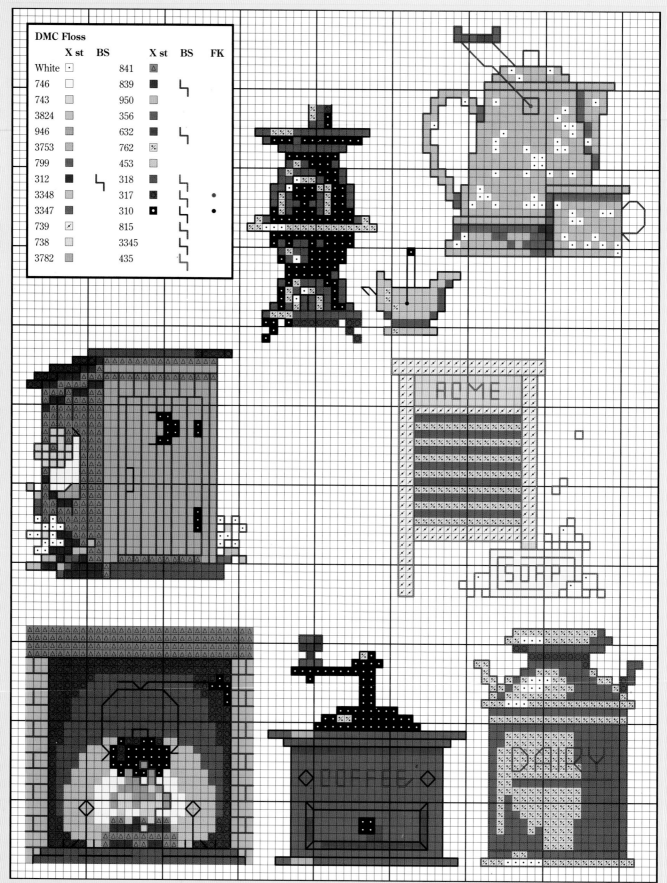

Hearth & Home

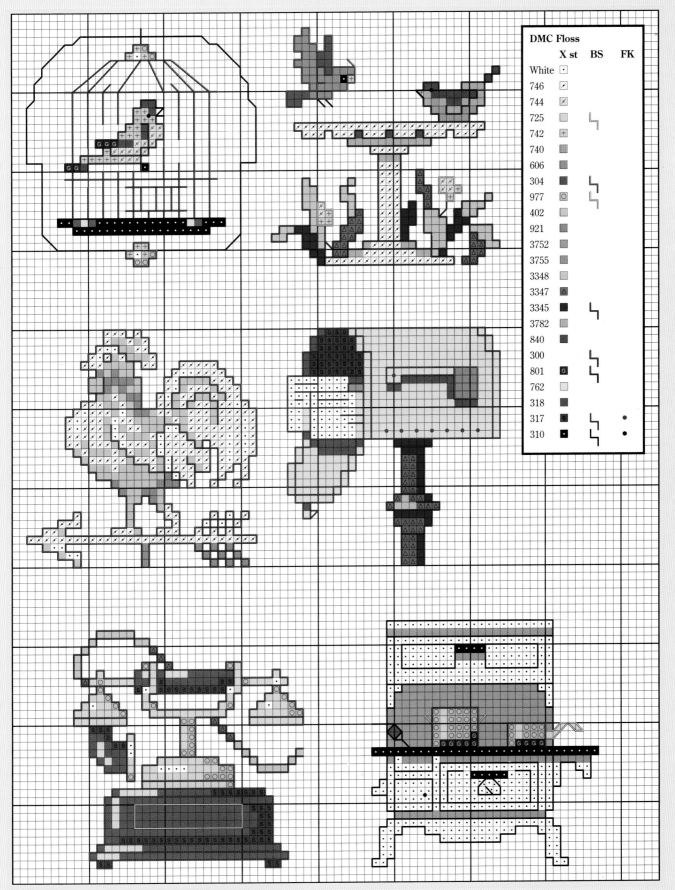

DMC Floss

	X st	BS	FK
White	·		
746	✗		
744	✗		
725		⌐	
742	+		
740			
606			
304		⌐	
977	◎		
402			
921			
3752			
3755			
3348			
3347	△		
3345		⌐	
3782			
840			
300		⌐	
801	G	⌐	
762			
318			
317	S	⌐	•
310	■	⌐	•

Hearth & Home

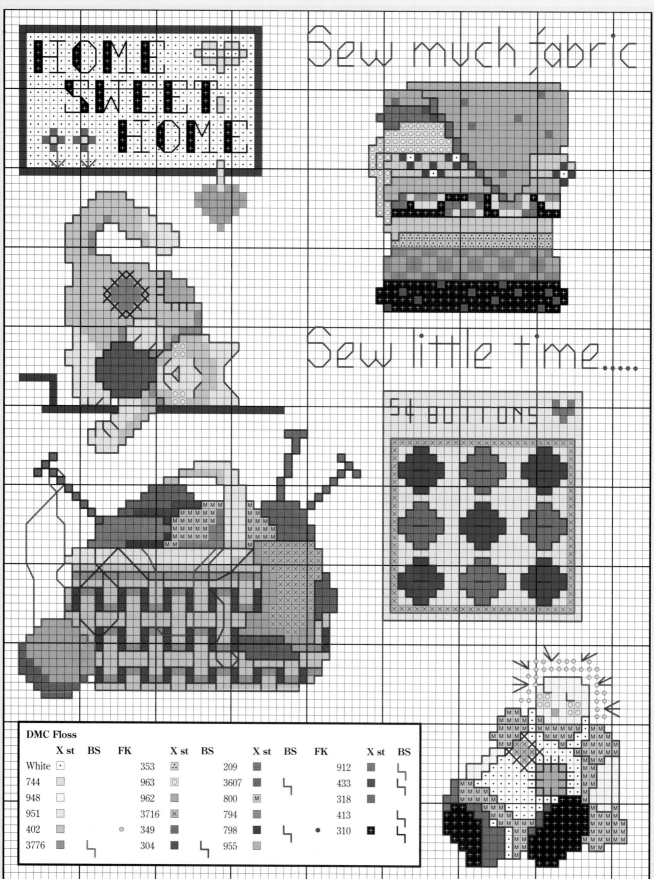

DMC Floss

	X st	BS	FK		X st	BS		X st	BS	FK		X st	BS
White	·			353				209				912		
744				963				3607				433		
948				962				800				318		
951				3716				794				413		
402			349				798			310			
3776				304				955						

Hearth & Home

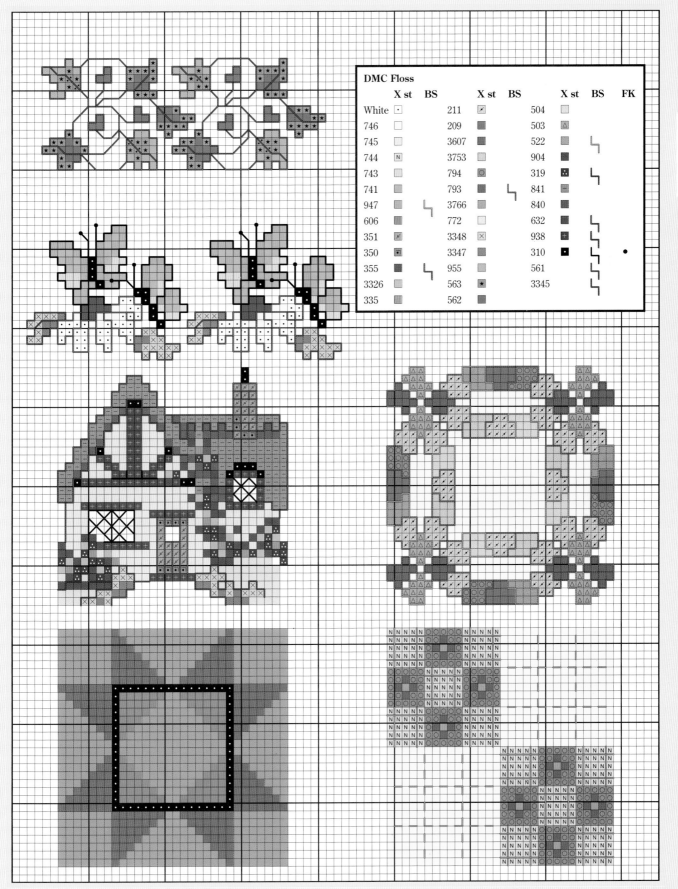

DMC Floss

	X st	BS		X st	BS		X st	BS	FK
White	·		211			504			
746			209			503	△		
745			3607			522		⌐	
744	N		3753			904			
743			794	⊙		319		⌐	
741			793		⌐	841			
947		⌐	3766			840			
606			772			632		⌐	
351	◿		3348	⊠		938	+	⌐	
350			3347			310		⌐	•
355		⌐	955			561		⌐	
3326			563	★		3345			
335			562						

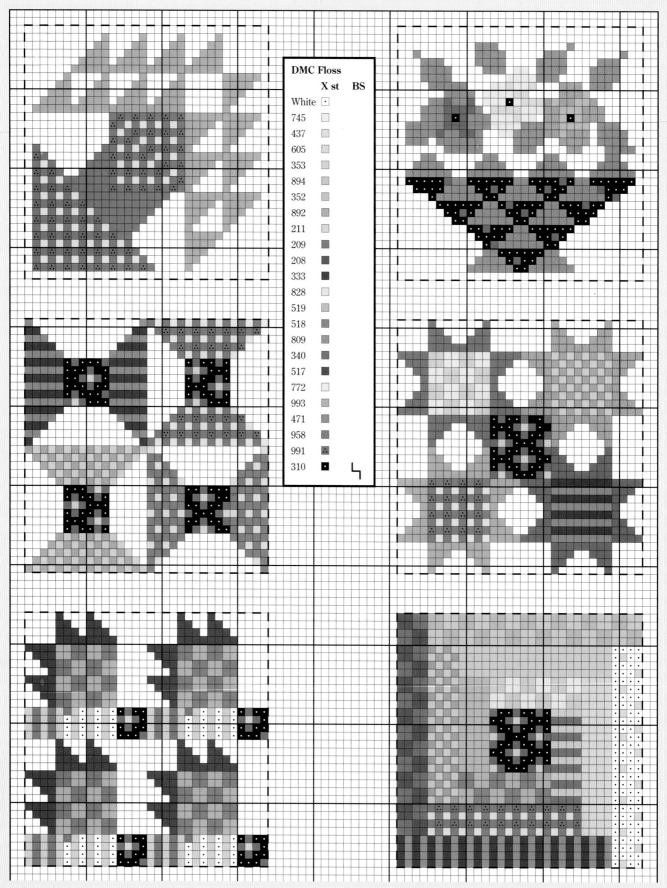

DMC Floss

	X st	BS
White	·	
745		
437		
605		
353		
894		
352		
892		
211		
209		
208		
333		
828		
519		
518		
809		
340		
517		
772		
993		
471		
958		
991		
310		

Hearth & Home

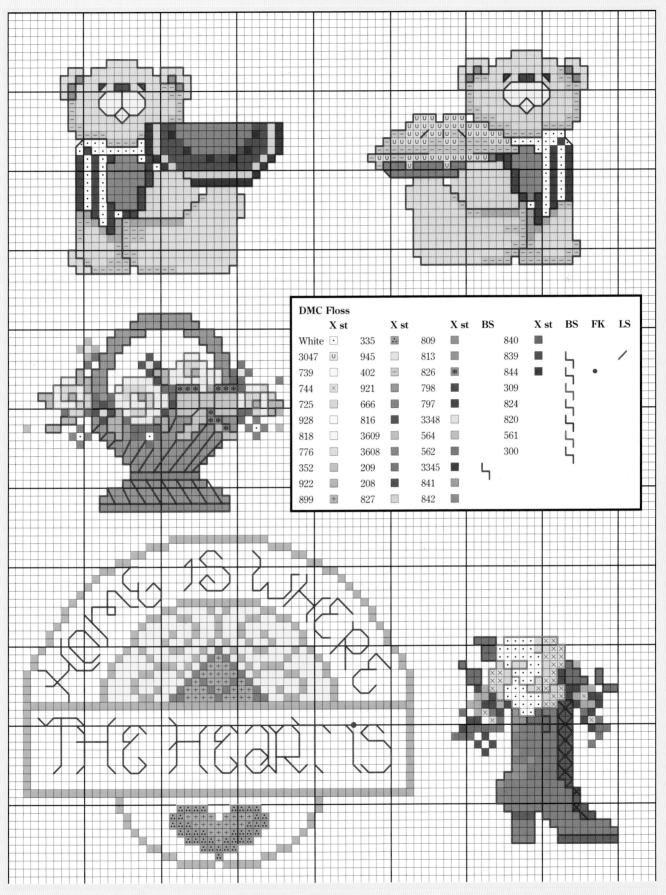

DMC Floss

	X st		X st		X st	BS		X st	BS	FK	LS
White	·	335		809		840					/
3047	U	945		813		839					
739		402	–	826	*	844					
744	✕	921		798		309					
725		666		797		824					
928		816		3348		820					
818		3609		564		561					
776		3608		562		300					
352		209		3345							
922		208		841							
899	+	827		842							

Heaven
&
Nature

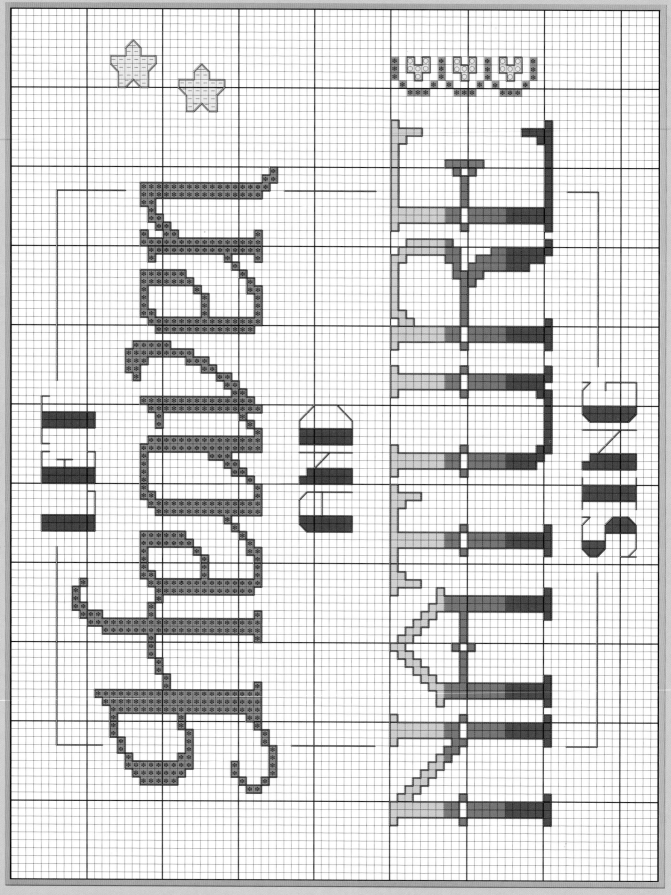

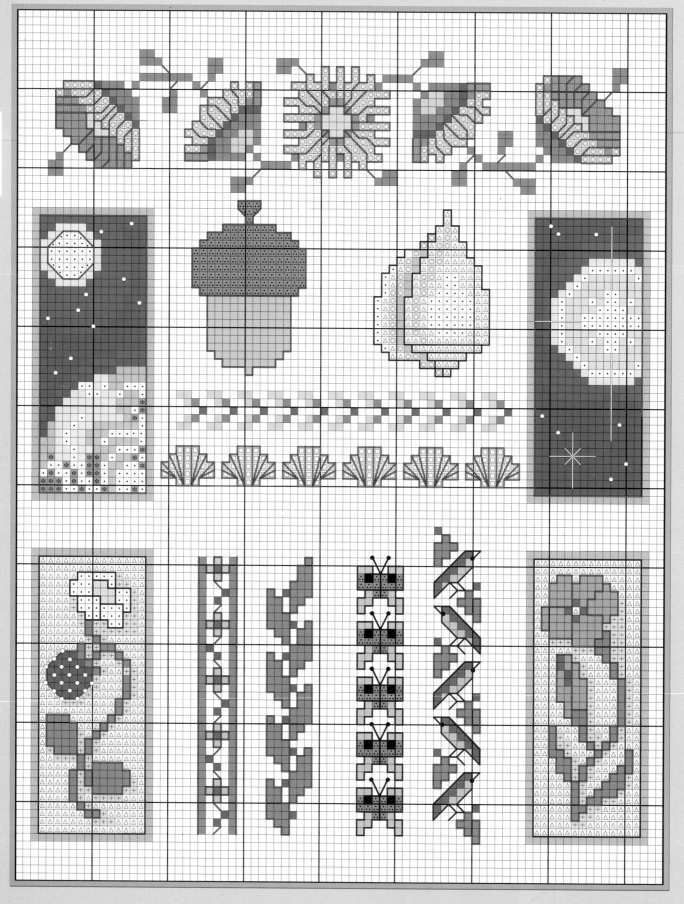

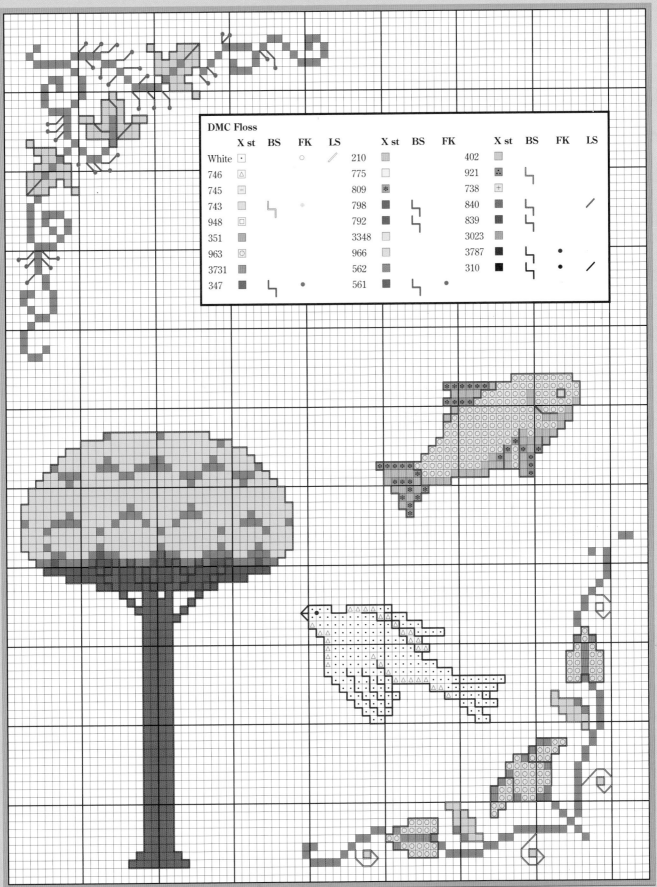

DMC Floss

	X st	BS	FK	LS		X st	BS	FK		X st	BS	FK	LS
White	·		○	/	210				402				
746	△				775				921		⌐		
745	⊟				809	✳			738	+			
743		⌐	·		798		⌐		840		⌐		/
948	▣				792		⌐		839		⌐		
351					3348				3023				
963	◉				966				3787		⌐	·	
3731					562				310		⌐	·	/
347		⌐	·		561		⌐	·					

88
8

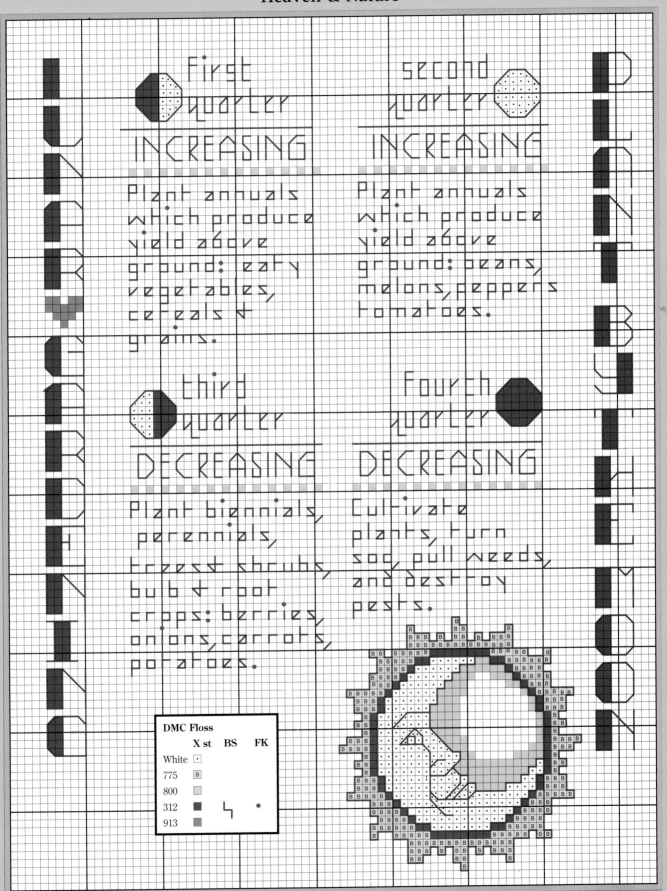

First quarter

INCREASING

Plant annuals which produce yield above ground: leafy vegetables, cereals & grains.

Second quarter

INCREASING

Plant annuals which produce yield above ground: beans, melons, peppers, tomatoes.

third quarter

DECREASING

Plant biennials, perennials, trees & shrubs, bulb & root crops: berries, onions, carrots, potatoes.

Fourth quarter

DECREASING

Cultivate plants, turn sod, pull weeds and destroy pests.

DMC Floss

	X st	BS	FK
White	·		
775	B		
800			
312	■	⌐	·
913			

DMC Floss

	X st		X st	BS		X st	BS		X st	BS		X st			X st	BS
White	·	970	◎		498			701			911		414			
712		721			3609	△		369			738	✗	310	△		
3822		720			519			320			3828		561			
743	+	3350			825			367			434		400			
741		666			704			966	G		415		413			

DMC Floss

X st		X st		X st		BS	X st		BS	X st		BS	X st		BS		BS
White	·	721		209			966			367			762			561		
712		3776	×	208			472			911			415			400		
3822		3733		327			704			738			414			413		
743	+	3350		959	B		702		G	3828			310	▲				
722	⊙	498		992			320			434			986					

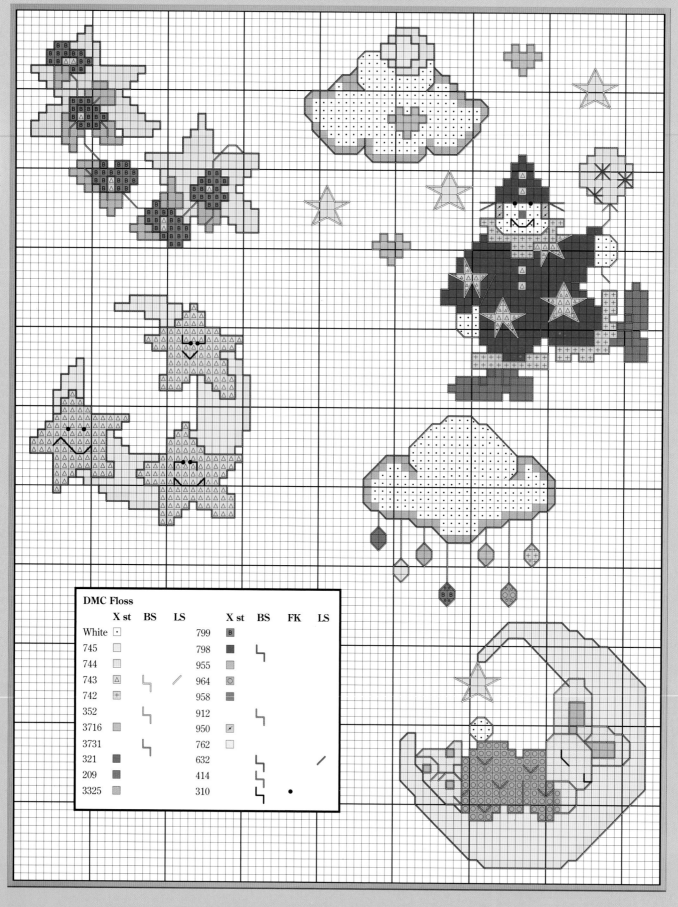

DMC Floss

	X st	BS	LS		X st	BS	FK	LS
White	·			799	B			
745				798		⌐		
744				955				
743	△	⌐	/	964	◎			
742	+			958				
352		⌐		912		⌐		
3716				950	◹	⌐		
3731		⌐		762		⌐		
321				632		⌐		/
209				414		⌐		
3325				310		⌐	•	

Heaven & Nature

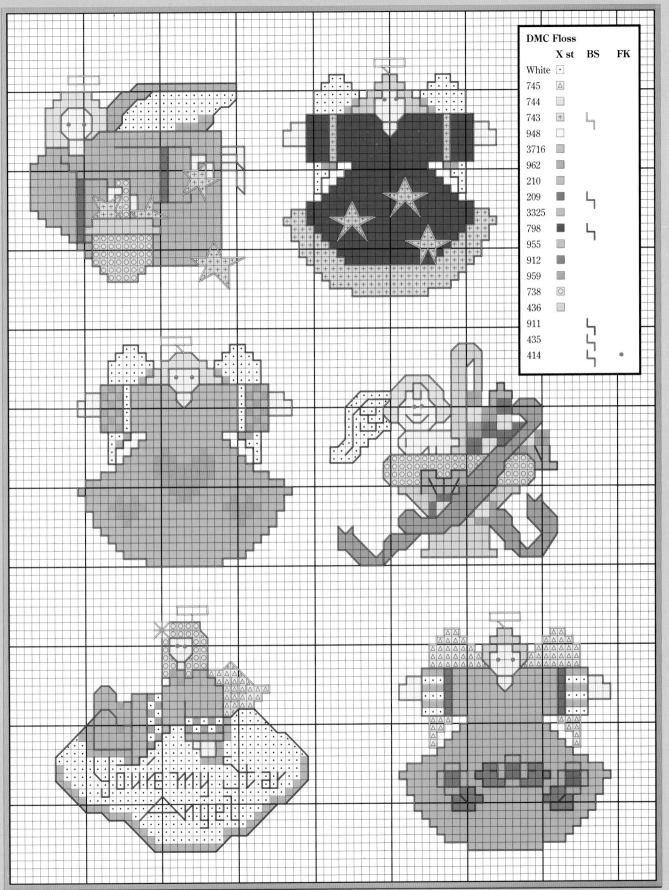

DMC Floss

	X st	BS	FK
White	·		
745	△		
744			
743	+	⌐	
948			
3716			
962			
210			
209		⌐	
3325			
798		⌐	
955			
912			
959			
738	○		
436			
911		⌐	
435		⌐	
414		⌐	·

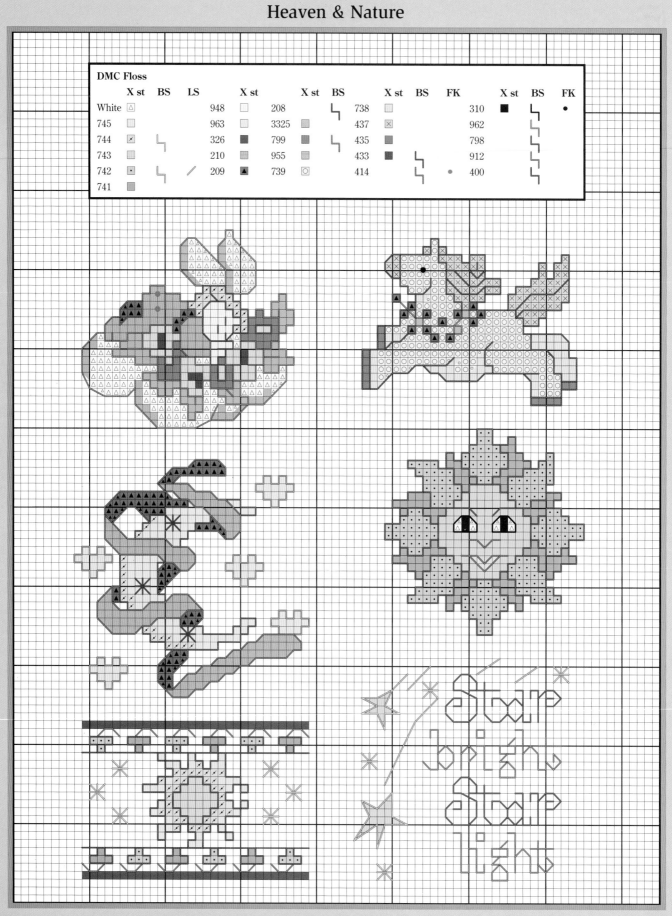

DMC Floss

	X st	BS	LS		X st		X st	BS		X st	BS	FK		X st	BS	FK
White	△			948		208			738			310	■		•
745				963		3325			437	⊠		962			
744				326		799			435			798			
743				210		955			433			912			
742		/	209	▲	739	◉		414	•	400			
741															

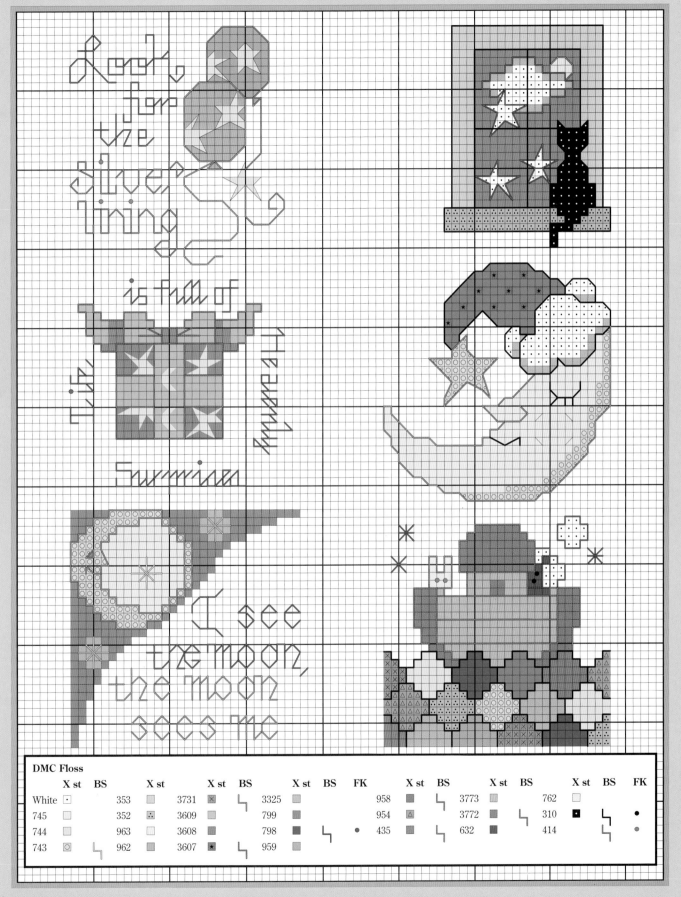

DMC Floss																		
	X st	BS		X st		X st	BS		X st	BS	FK		X st	BS		X st	BS	
White	·		353		3731	⊠		3325				958			3773		762		
745			352		3609		799					954	△		3772		310	■	•
744			963		3608		798		•	435				632		414		•
743	◉		962		3607	★	959												

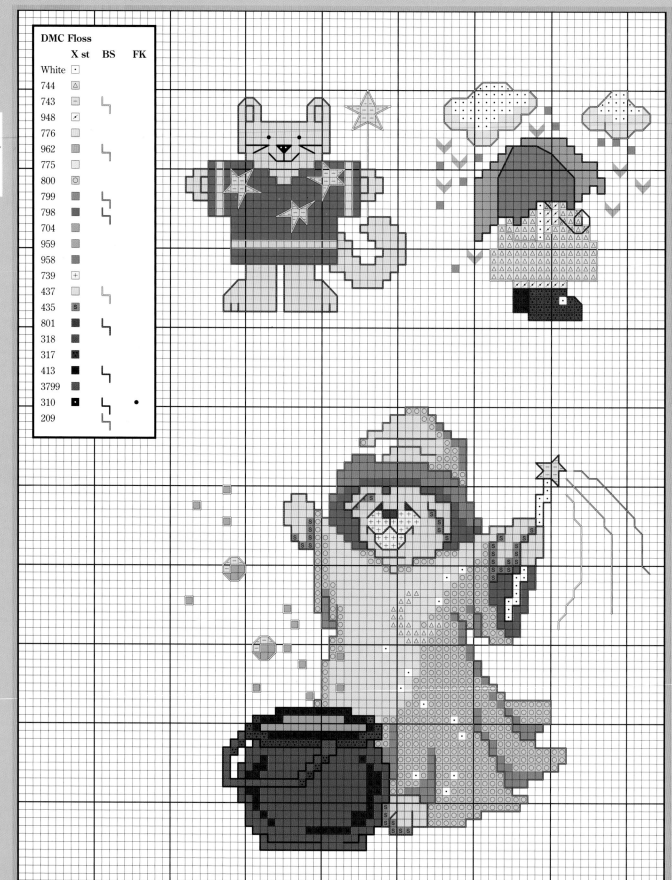

DMC Floss

	X st	BS	FK
White	·		
744	△		
743	−	⌐	
948	⚹		
776			
962		⌐	
775			
800	⊙		
799		⌐	
798		⌐	
704			
959			
958			
739	+		
437		⌐	
435	S		
801		⌐	
318			
317			
413		⌐	
3799			
310	·	⌐	•
209		⌐	

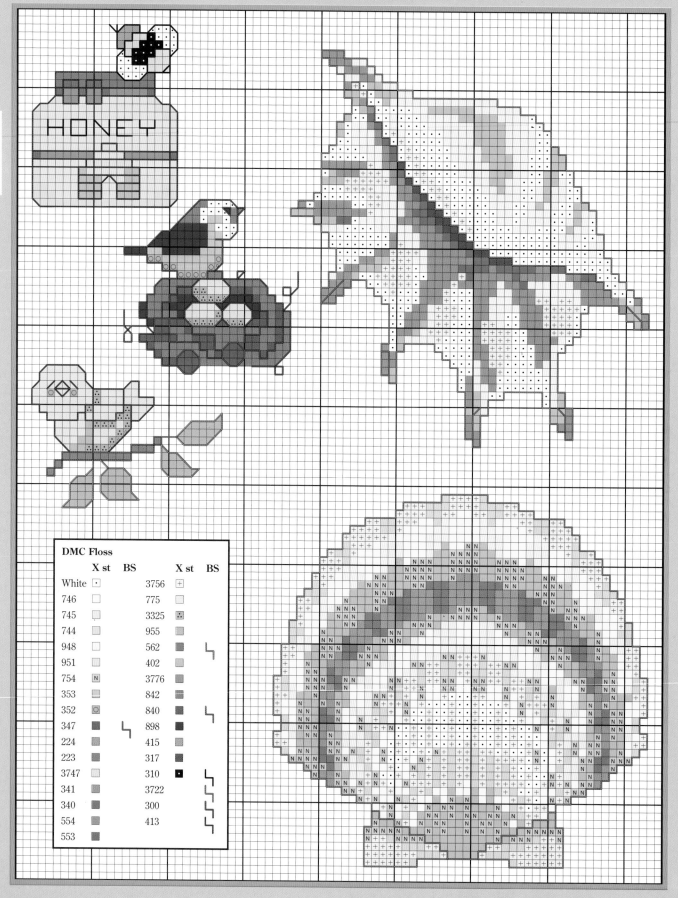

DMC Floss

	X st	BS		X st	BS
White	·		3756	⊞	
746			775		
745			3325	⊡	
744			955		
948			562		⌐
951			402		
754	N		3776		
353			842		
352	○		840		⌐
347		⌐	898		
224			415		
223			317		
3747			310	■	⌐
341			3722		⌐
340			300		⌐
554			413		⌐
553					

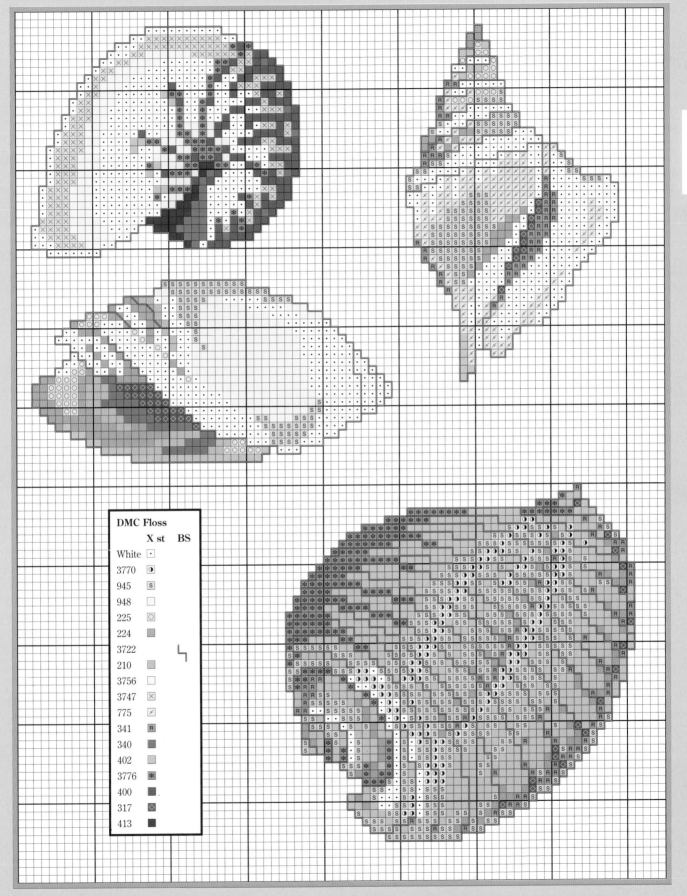

DMC Floss

	X st	BS
White	·	
3770	◐	
945	S	
948	☐	
225	○	
224	▨	
3722		⌐
210	▨	
3756	☐	
3747	✕	
775	✗	
341	R	
340	▧	
402	▨	
3776	✳	
400	▨	
317	◇	
413	■	

DMC Floss

	X st		X st	BS		X st	BS
White	·	225		368			
745	△	224		320			
743		223		911			
676	⊠	221		434			
722		554		816			
3776	+	552		367			
3716		966	G	561			
349		3817		400			

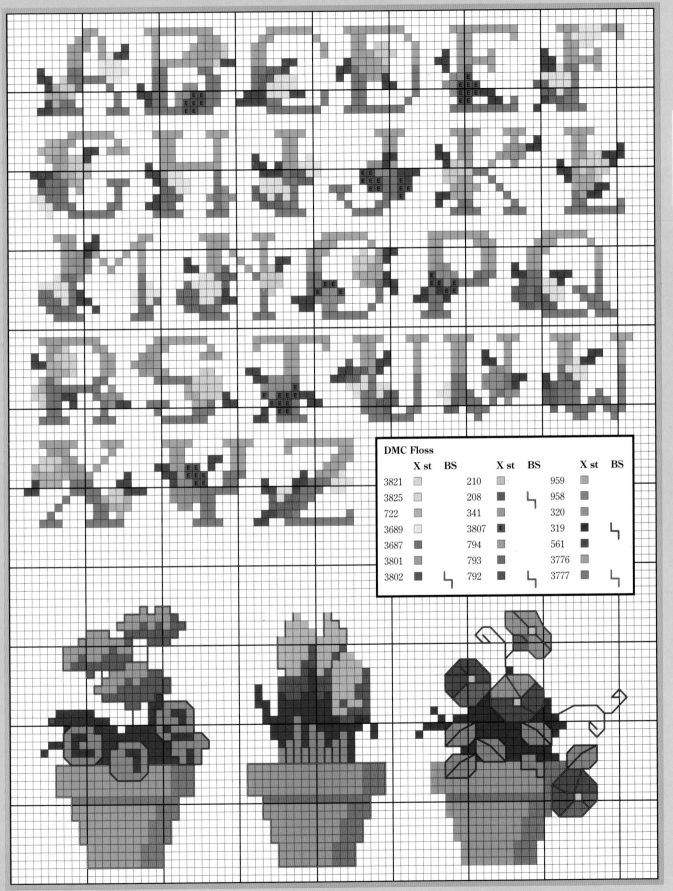

DMC Floss

	X st	BS		X st	BS		X st	BS
3821			210			959		
3825			208		⌐	958		
722			341			320		
3689			3807	E		319		⌐
3687			794			561		
3801			793			3776		
3802		⌐	792		⌐	3777		⌐

Happy
Holidays

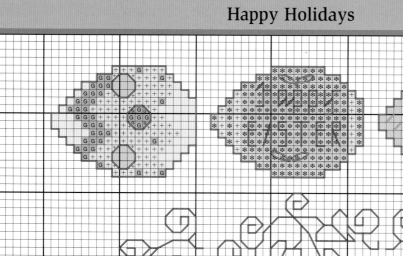

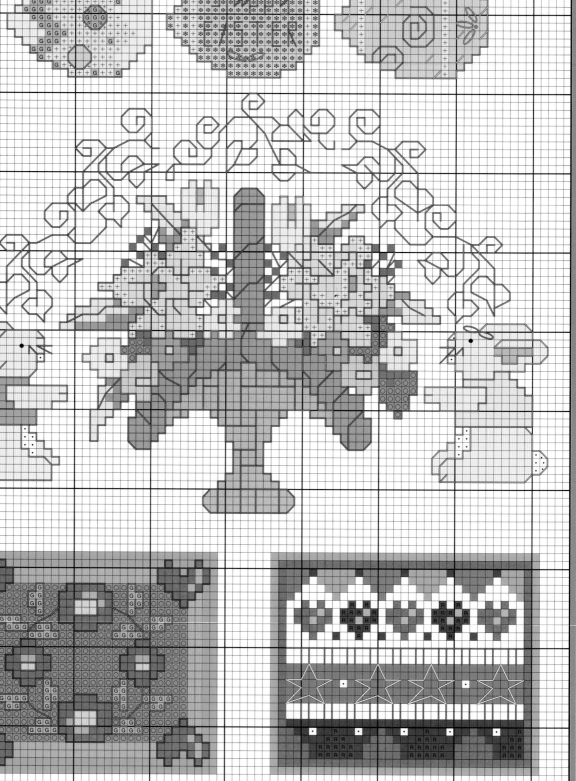

Happy Holidays

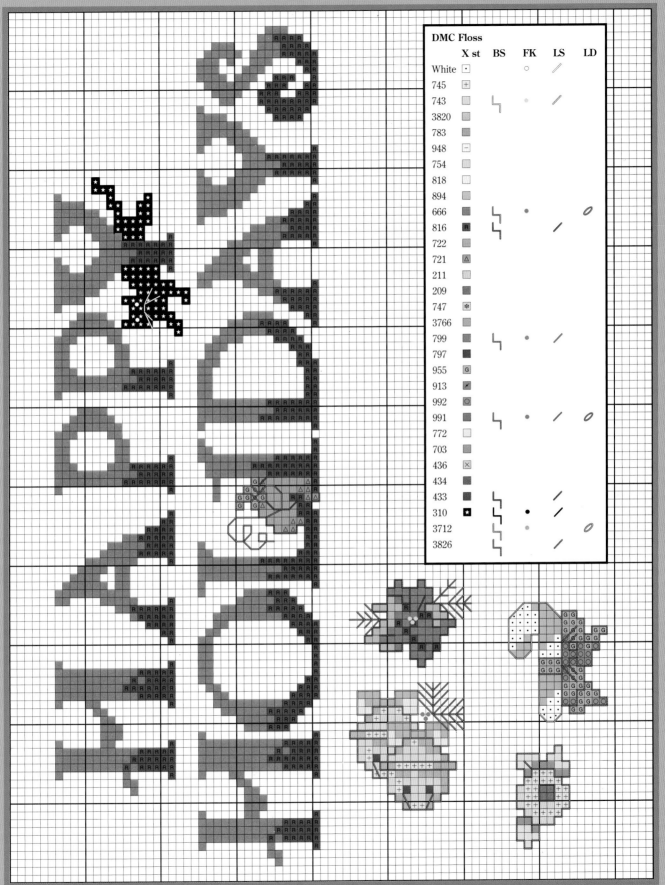

DMC Floss

	X st	BS	FK	LS	LD
White	·		○	/	
745	+				
743		⌐	·	/	
3820					
783					
948	–				
754					
818					
894					
666		⌐	·		⊘
816	R	⌐		/	
722					
721	△				
211					
209					
747	✳				
3766					
799		⌐	·	/	
797					
955	G				
913	➚				
992	⊙				
991		⌐	·	/	⊘
772					
703					
436	⊠				
434					
433		⌐		/	
310	✪	⌐	●	/	
3712		⌐	·		⊘
3826		⌐		/	

Happy Holidays

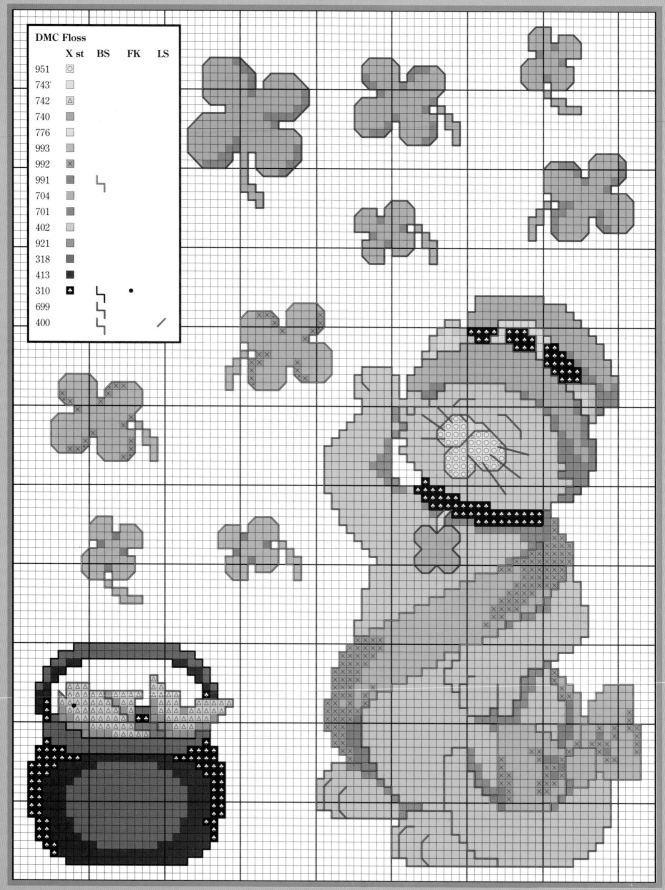

DMC Floss

	X st	BS	FK	LS
951	⊙			
743				
742	△			
740				
776				
993				
992	✕			
991		⌐		
704				
701				
402				
921				
318				
413				
310	✿	⌐	•	
699		⌐		
400		⌐		/

Happy Holidays

DMC Floss

	X st		X st	BS	LS		X st	BS	FK
White	·	209	⊠			413	■	⌐	•
353		208	■	⌐		310	■	⌐	
963		3761				351		⌐	
3716	R	334				3350		⌐	•
961		959		⌐		943		⌐	
211		415		⌐	/				

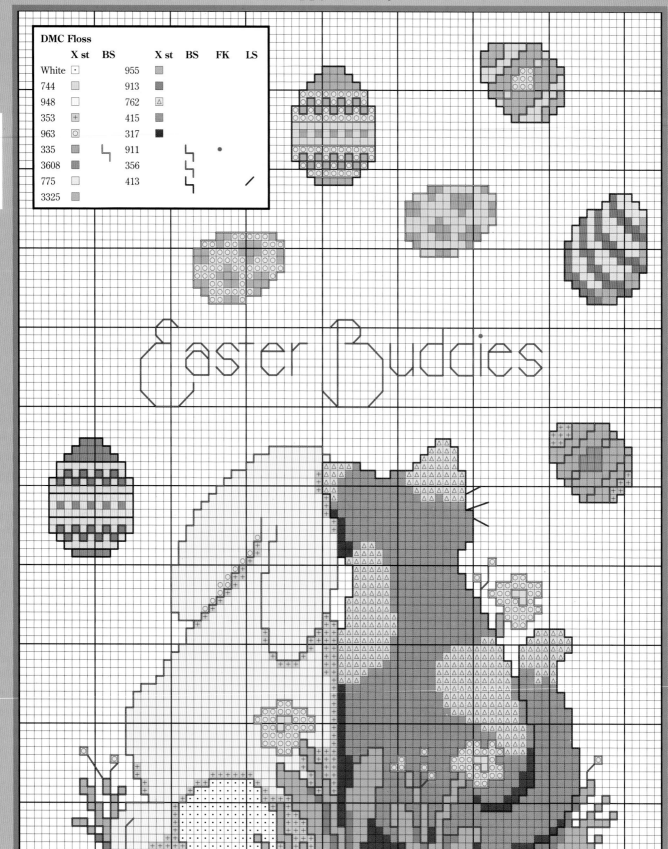

DMC Floss

	X st	BS		X st	BS	FK	LS
White	·		955				
744			913				
948			762	△			
353	+		415				
963	⊙		317				
335		⌐	911		⌐		
3608			356		⌐		
775			413		⌐	•	/
3325							

Easter Buddies

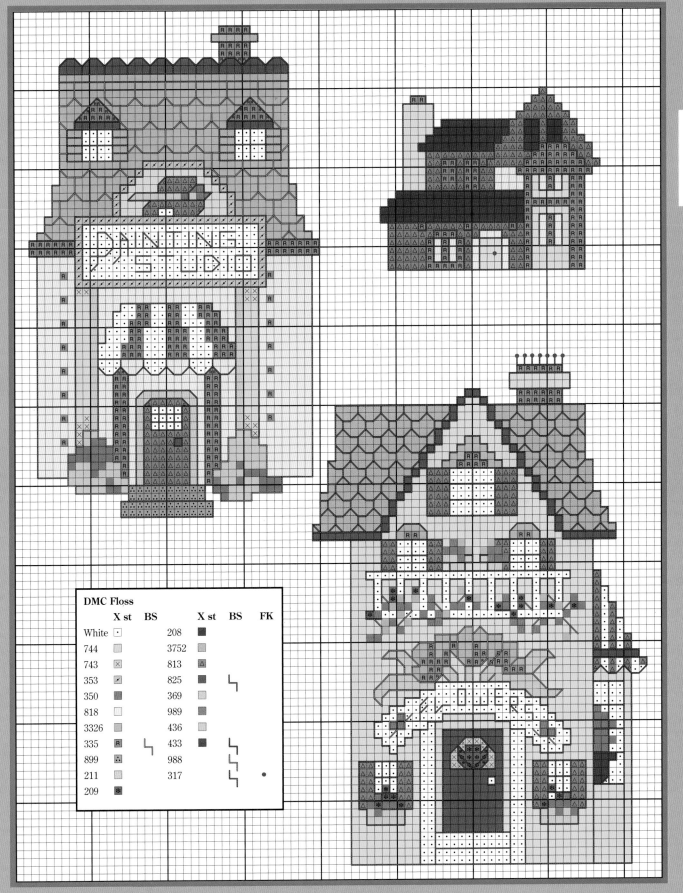

DMC Floss

	X st	BS		X st	BS	FK
White	·		208	▣		
744	▫		3752	▨		
743	✕		813	△		
353	◪		825	▨	⌐	
350	▨		369	▨		
818	▫		989	▨		
3326	▨		436	▨		
335	R	⌐	433	▨	⌐	
899	⦂		988		⌐	
211	▨		317		⌐	•
209	✳					

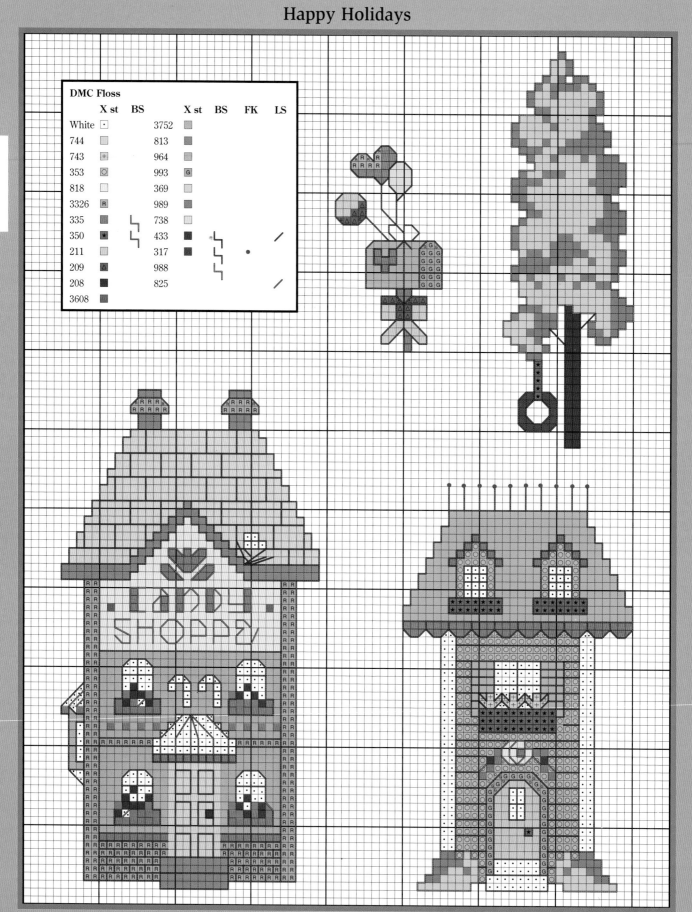

DMC Floss

	X st	BS		X st	BS	FK	LS
White	·		3752				
744			813				
743	+		964				
353	○		993	G			
818			369				
3326	R		989				
335			738				
350	★		433				
211			317			·	
209	△		988				
208			825				
3608							

Happy Holidays

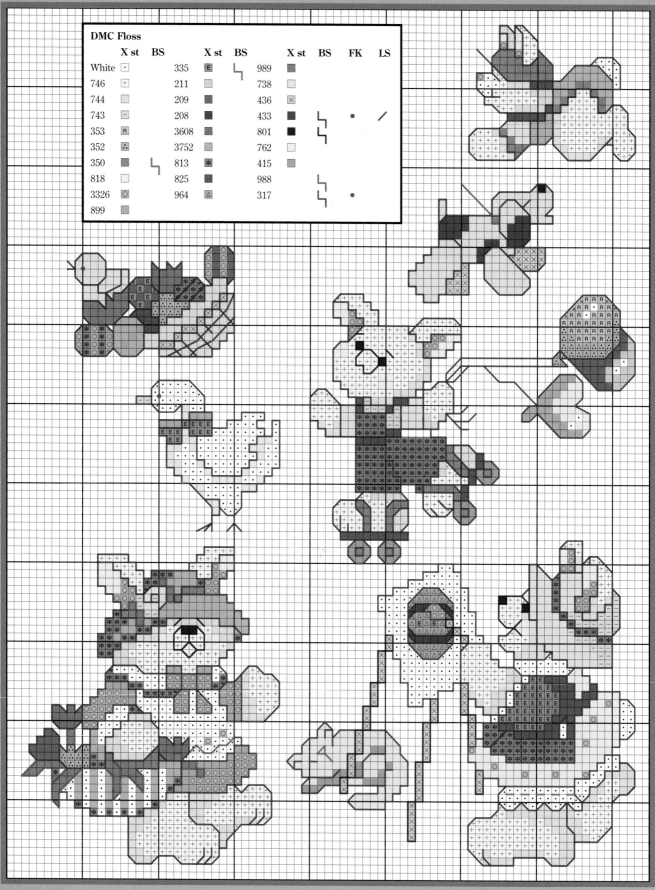

DMC Floss

	X st	BS		X st	BS		X st	BS	FK	LS
White	·		335	E	⌐	989				
746	+		211			738				
744			209			436	⊠			
743	−		208			433		⌐	•	╱
353	R		3608			801				
352	⊠		3752			762				
350		⌐	813	✳		415				
818			825			988		⌐		
3326	◎		964	△		317		⌐	•	
899										

Happy Holidays

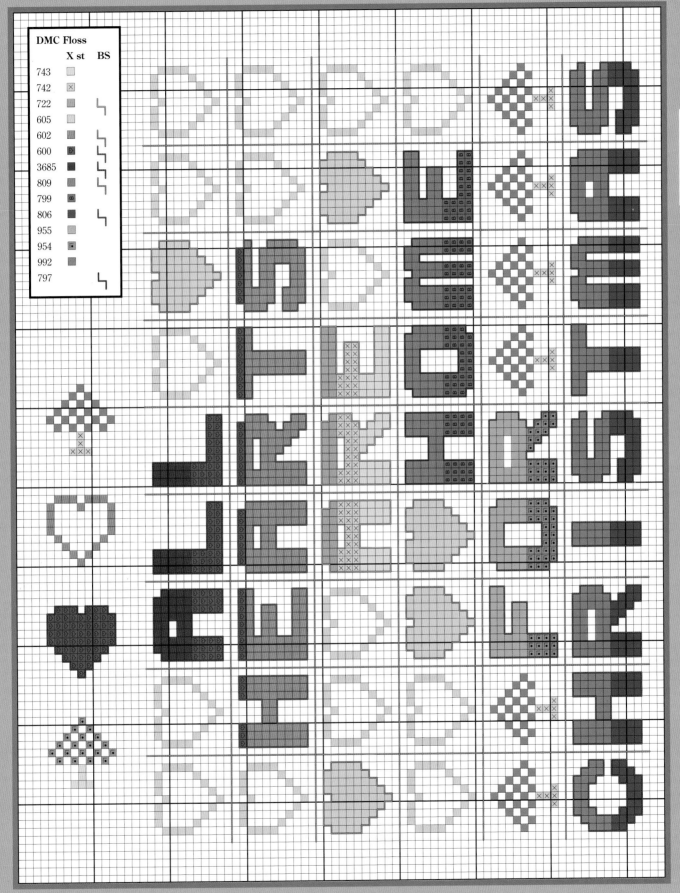

DMC Floss

	X st	BS
743		
742		
722		⌐
605		
602		⌐
600		⌐
3685		⌐
809		⌐
799		
806		⌐
955		
954		
992		
797		⌐

Happy Holidays

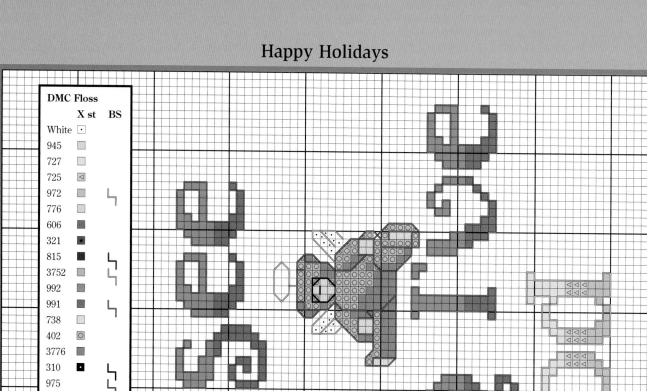

DMC Floss

	X st	BS
White	·	
945		
727		
725	◁	
972		⌐
776		
606		
321	✶	
815		⌐
3752		⌐
992		⌐
991		⌐
738		
402	◎	
3776		
310	■	⌐
975		⌐

Happy Holidays

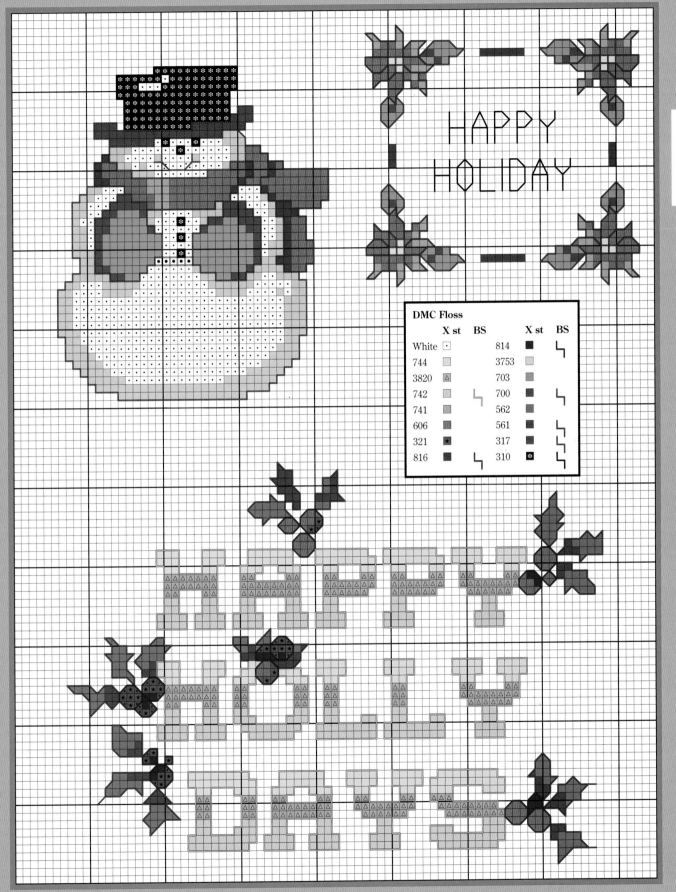

DMC Floss

	X st	BS		X st	BS
White	·		814	■	
744			3753		
3820	△		703		
742		⌐	700		⌐
741			562		
606			561		⌐
321	★		317		⌐
816		⌐	310	✳	⌐

Happy Holidays

DMC Floss

	X st		X st	BS		X st	BS
White	·	666	⊠	⌐	3777		
445		3753			921		⌐
726	▨	3325			762		
963		322			415	◉	
3716	◪	704			414		⌐
962		700		⌐	310	✳	⌐
351		402			317		⌐
606		3776					

Happy Holidays

DMC Floss		
	X st	BS
White	·	
726		
741		
818		
606		
816		⌐
3753		
703		
700		⌐
317		⌐
310	✳	⌐

Happy Holidays

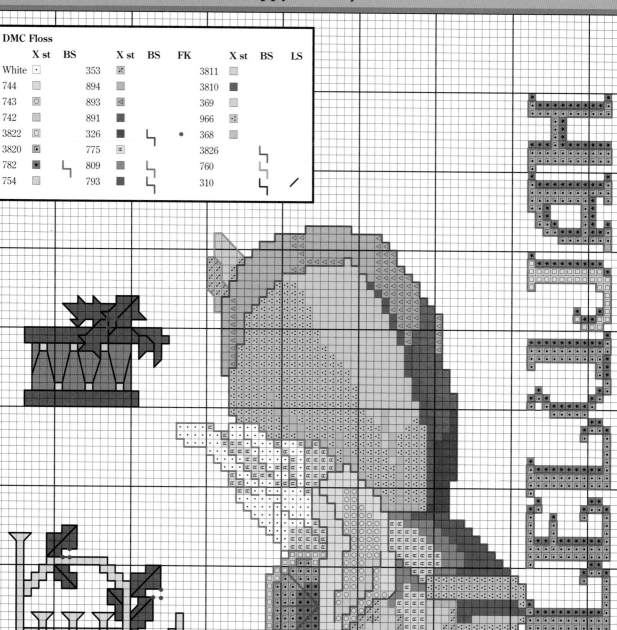

DMC Floss

	X st	BS		X st	BS	FK		X st	BS	LS
White	·		353				3811			
744			894				3810			
743			893				369			
742			891				966			
3822			326		⌐	•	368			
3820			775	R			3826			
782	★	⌐	809				760		⌐	
754		⌐	793		⌐		310		⌐	╱

DMC Floss

	X st	BS		X st	BS
744			552		⌐
742	+	⌐	800		
604			799		⌐
602		⌐	3807		⌐
666		⌐	3819		
498			704		⌐
209			783		⌐

Happy Holidays

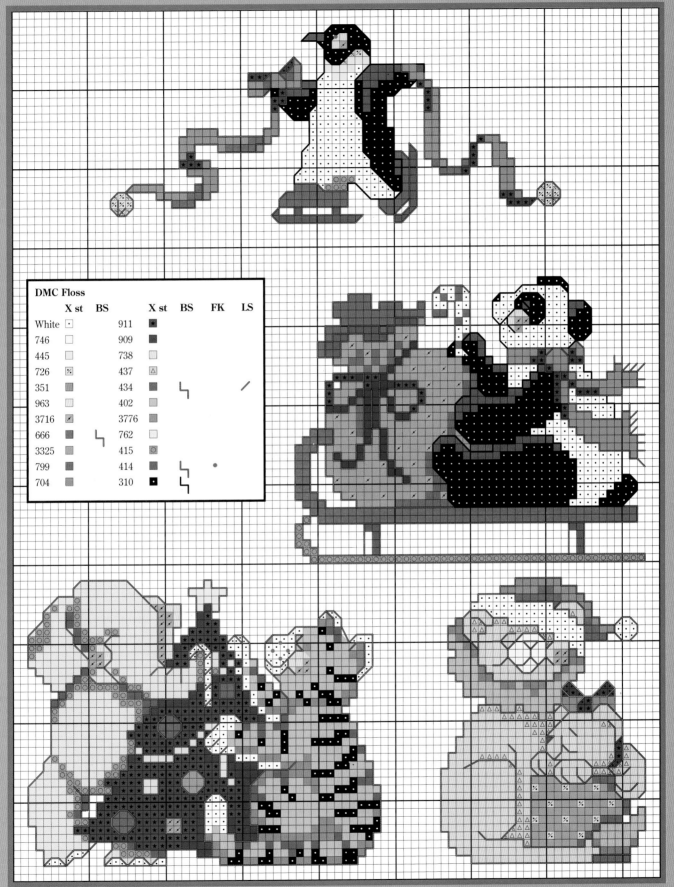

DMC Floss

	X st	BS		X st	BS	FK	LS
White	·		911	★			
746			909				
445			738				
726	⧂		437	△			
351			434		⌐		╱
963			402				
3716	⚋		3776				
666		⌐	762				
3325			415	⊙			
799			414		⌐	•	
704			310	⊡			⌐

Happy Holidays

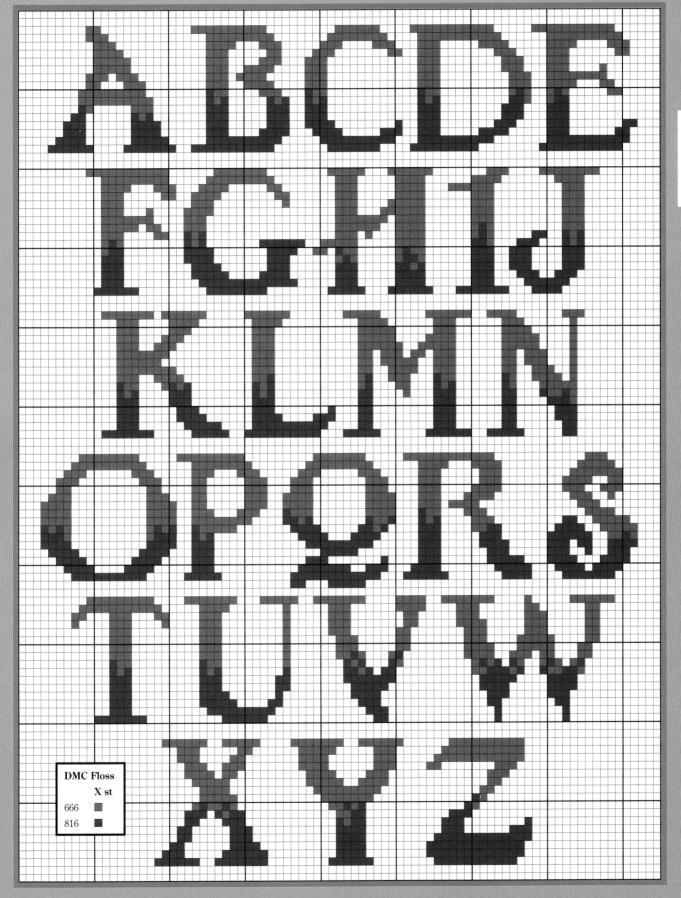

DMC Floss
X st

666
816

Metric Equivalency

MM-Millimetres   CM-Centimetres

INCHES TO MILLIMETRES AND CENTIMETRES

INCHES	MM	CM	INCHES	CM	INCHES	CM
⅛	3	0.3	9	22.9	30	76.2
¼	6	0.6	10	25.4	31	78.7
½	13	1.3	12	30.5	33	83.8
⅝	16	1.6	13	33.0	34	86.4
¾	19	1.9	14	35.6	35	88.9
⅞	22	2.2	15	38.1	36	91.4
1	25	2.5	16	40.6	37	94.0
1¼	32	3.2	17	43.2	38	96.5
1½	38	3.8	18	45.7	39	99.1
1¾	44	4.4	19	48.3	40	101.6
2	51	5.1	20	50.8	41	104.1
2½	64	6.4	21	53.3	42	106.7
3	76	7.6	22	55.9	43	109.2
3½	89	8.9	23	58.4	44	111.8
4	102	10.2	24	61.0	45	114.3
4½	114	11.4	25	63.5	46	116.8
5	127	12.7	26	66.0	47	119.4
6	152	15.2	27	68.6	48	121.9
7	178	17.8	28	71.1	49	124.5
8	203	20.3	29	73.7	50	127.0

YARDS TO METRES

YARDS	METRES	YARDS	METRES	YARDS	METRES	YARDS	METRES	YARDS	METRES
⅛	0.11	2⅛	1.94	4⅛	3.77	6⅛	5.60	8⅛	7.43
¼	0.23	2¼	2.06	4¼	3.89	6¼	5.72	8¼	7.54
⅜	0.34	2⅜	2.17	4⅜	4.00	6⅜	5.83	8⅜	7.66
½	0.46	2½	2.29	4½	4.11	6½	5.94	8½	7.77
⅝	0.57	2⅝	2.40	4⅝	4.23	6⅝	6.06	8⅝	7.89
¾	0.69	2¾	2.51	4¾	4.34	6¾	6.17	8¾	8.00
⅞	0.80	2⅞	2.63	4⅞	4.46	6⅞	6.29	8⅞	8.12
1	0.91	3	2.74	5	4.57	7	6.40	9	8.23
1⅛	1.03	3⅛	2.86	5⅛	4.69	7⅛	6.52	9⅛	8.34
1¼	1.14	3¼	2.97	5¼	4.80	7¼	6.63	9¼	8.46
1⅜	1.26	3⅜	3.09	5⅜	4.91	7⅜	6.74	9⅜	8.57
1½	1.37	3½	3.20	5½	5.03	7½	6.86	9½	8.69
1⅝	1.49	3⅝	3.31	5⅝	5.14	7⅝	6.97	9⅝	8.80
1¾	1.60	3¾	3.43	5¾	5.26	7¾	7.09	9¾	8.92
1⅞	1.71	3⅞	3.54	5⅞	5.37	7⅞	7.20	9⅞	9.03
2	1.83	4	3.66	6	5.49	8	7.32	10	9.14

Index